DATE DUE

BEYOND CORPORATE SOCIAL RESPONSIBILITY

Corporate Social Responsibility (CSR) has emerged as an important approach for addressing the social and environmental impact of company activities. Yet companies are increasingly expected to go beyond this. They are now often expected to assist in addressing many of the world's most pressing problems, including climate change, poverty and HIV/Aids. With increasing expectations placed on business, this book asks if CSR is capable of delivering on these larger expectations. It does so by investigating an industry that has been at the centre of the CSR development – the oil and gas sector. Looking at companies from developed countries such as Exxon and Shell, as well as companies from emerging economies such as Brazil's Petrobras and China's CNOOC, the book investigates the potential of CSR for addressing three important challenges in the business–society relationship: the environment, development and governance.

JEDRZEJ GEORGE FRYNAS is Professor of Corporate Social Responsibility and Strategic Management at Middlesex University Business School, and Honorary Senior Research Fellow at Birmingham Business School, University of Birmingham. He has wide experience in executive education at six different UK universities and leads training courses on CSR for managers and public sector decision-makers in conjunction with a leading responsible business consultancy Article 13. He has published widely in journals such as International Affairs, Strategic Management Journal and Third World Quarterly. His books include *Oil in Nigeria* (2000) and *Global Strategic Management* (2005).

Beyond Corporate Social Responsibility

OIL MULTINATIONALS AND SOCIAL CHALLENGES

Jedrzej George Frynas

CAMBRIDGE
UNIVERSITY PRESS

CAMBRIDGE UNIVERSITY PRESS
Cambridge, New York, Melbourne, Madrid, Cape Town, Singapore,
São Paulo, Delhi, Dubai, Tokyo, Mexico City

Cambridge University Press
The Edinburgh Building, Cambridge CB2 8RU, UK

Published in the United States of America by Cambridge University Press, New York

www.cambridge.org
Information on this title: www.cambridge.org/9780521868440

First published 2009

A catalogue record for this publication is available from the British Library

ISBN 978-0-521-86844-0 Hardback

Contents

Figures

Tables

ONE

Introduction

Companies are increasingly expected to assist in addressing many of the world's pressing problems including climate change, poverty and HIV/Aids. According to a 2007 survey by the consultancy firm McKinsey carried out among the chief executive officers (CEOs) of companies, 95 per cent of those questioned believe that society has greater expectations than it did five years ago that companies will assume public responsibilities. More than half of the CEOs believe that these expectations will further increase significantly during the next five years (Bielak *et al.* 2007).

Corporate Social Responsibility (CSR) has emerged as a business approach for addressing the social and environmental impact of company activities. With increasing expectations placed on business, one needs to ask if CSR is able to fulfil these larger expectations. Therefore, the aim of this book is to analyse CSR's potential and limitations for contributing towards wider societal 'challenges'.

The central part of the book investigates the potential of CSR for addressing three challenges in the business–society relationship: the environment, development and governance. The book suggests that CSR has some potential for dealing with environmental issues such as carbon emissions and oil spills. Yet, in general, the current CSR agenda largely fails to deal with the three challenges, and a number of important economic and political issues are not yet addressed. The book explains the existing constraints to CSR and provides some recommendations in the conclusion.

The author firmly believes that any discussion of the CSR agenda must have a solid basis in reality. Too many books on CSR are based on superficial examples and unfounded arguments. Too many books fail to appreciate the importance of context in the evolution of CSR. That is why this book has focused in greater depth on companies from a single industry: the oil and gas sector, which includes two of the world's leaders in the CSR movement: Shell and BP. Throughout the book we also look at companies from developing nations such as Brazil's Petrobras and South Africa's Sasol. Business now operates in a global arena and companies from the so-called emerging markets such as China, India and Brazil are increasingly expected to make social and environmental contributions.

The book is based on more than ten years' experience in researching the oil and gas industry, and the author has had hundreds of conversations with oil company staff, civil society advocates, government officials, consultants, development specialists, journalists and local people around these issues.[1] The author has published widely on CSR and leads CSR training courses for managers and public sector decision-makers in conjunction with a consultancy firm. The lessons from this research are general and go beyond the oil and gas industry.

What is CSR?

In order to understand the meaning of contemporary CSR, it is useful to go back in time. While CSR is a recent term, preoccupation with

---

[1] In the course of this research, the author has interviewed staff from the following multinational oil companies: Shell, BP, Exxon, Chevron, Total, Agip, Statoil, BG Group, Petrobras and PDVSA.

business ethics and the social dimensions of business activity has a long history. Business practices based on moral principles and 'controlled greed' were advocated by pre-Christian Western thinkers such as Cicero in the first century BC and their non-Western equivalents such as the Indian statesman and philosopher Kautilya in the fourth century BC, while Islam and the medieval Christian church publicly condemned certain business practices, notably usury.

The modern precursors of CSR can be traced back to the nineteenth-century boycotts of foodstuffs produced with slave labour, the moral vision of business leaders such as Cadbury and Salt, who promoted the social welfare of their workers, and the Nuremberg war crimes trials after the Second World War, which saw the directors of the German firm I. G. Farben found guilty of mass murder and slavery (Ciulla 1991; Pegg 2003; Sekhar 2002). From a historical perspective, CSR is simply the latest manifestation of earlier debates as to the role of business in society. What is new, according to Fabig and Boele, is that 'today's debates are conducted at the intersection of development, environment and human rights, and are more global in outlook than earlier in this century or even in the 1960s' (Fabig and Boele 1999).

While the role of business in society seems to have been changing for some time, there is no agreement among observers on what CSR stands for or where the boundaries of CSR lie. Different people have interpreted CSR differently. For example, CSR means different things to practitioners seeking to implement CSR inside companies than to researchers trying to establish CSR as a discipline. It can also mean something different to civil society groups than to the private sector.

The responsibilities of companies in developing nations are also defined differently depending on the social – especially national – context (Baskin 2006; Frynas 2006); for instance, CSR among Malaysian firms is partly motivated by religious notions and Islam's prescriptions of certain business practices (Zulkifli and Amran 2006); the specific flavour of CSR in Argentina can be partly attributed to

Argentina's economic crisis in December 2001 (Newell and Muro 2006); while companies in South Africa are forced to address racial inequality as a result of the unique legacy of apartheid (Fig 2005). Companies in Malaysia focus on charitable activities, especially around Muslim and Chinese religious holidays, while companies in South Africa focus on black empowerment schemes. Therefore, CSR or 'being socially responsible' clearly means different things to different people in different countries.

Although these differences in the understanding of CSR are perhaps inevitable given the wide range of issues that companies need to deal with, they can be frustrating, not least to company managers who might prefer a bounded concept similar to quality control or financial accounting. Instead, managers find themselves wrestling with issues as diverse as corporate governance, environmental management, corporate philanthropy, human rights, labour rights, health issues and community development. To complicate matters further, new terms have entered the vocabulary of business and civil society – concepts such as corporate accountability, stakeholder engagement and sustainable development, aimed variously at replacing, redefining or complementing the CSR concept (see Table 1.1 for an overview). Indeed, some companies now prefer to use terms such as 'sustainability' or 'citizenship' instead of CSR.

We should also be careful not to superimpose Western notions of CSR on the reality in developing countries. Philanthropy is a key example. In Europe, the notion of philanthropy was previously dismissed and often not regarded as part of CSR because it does not relate to the impact of the day-to-day operations of the firm. But firms are primarily expected to actively assist their local communities in many developing countries. When asked by the World Business Council for Sustainable Development (2000) how CSR should be defined, people in Ghana, for instance, stressed local community issues such as 'building local capacity' and 'filling-in when government falls short'. Studies on countries as diverse as Nigeria, Pakistan,

TABLE 1.1: *Multiple interpretations of Corporate Social Responsibility*

Interpretation	Relevant authors
Business ethics and morality	Bowie 1998; ; Freeman 1994; Phillips 1997, 2003; Phillips and Margolis 1999; Stark 1993
Corporate accountability	O'Dwyer 2005; Owen *et al.* 2000
Corporate citizenship	Andriof and Waddock 2002; Carroll 2004; Matten and Crane 2005
Corporate giving and philanthropy	Carroll 1991, 2004
Corporate greening and green marketing	Crane 2000; Hussain 1999; Saha and Darnton 2005
Diversity management	Kamp and Hagedorn-Rasmussen 2004
Environmental responsibility	DesJardins 1998; McGee 1998
Human rights	Cassel 2001; Welford 2002
Responsible buying and supply chain management	Drumwright 1994; Emmelhainz and Adams 1999; Graafland 2002
Socially responsible investment	Aslaksen and Synnestvedt 2003; Jayne and Skerratt 2003; McLaren 2004; Warhurst 2001
Stakeholder engagement	Donaldson and Preston 1995; Freeman 1984, 1994
Sustainability	Amaeshi and Crane 2006; Bansal 2005; Korhonen 2002

Source: Amaeshi and Adi 2007.

Malaysia and Argentina suggest that philanthropic activities are considered the main social responsibility of business in these countries (Ahmad 2006; Amaeshi *et al.* 2006; Newell and Muro 2006; Zulkifli and Amran 2006). Many philanthropic activities by business in developing countries are likely to be genuine and may be guided by traditional notions of business obligations with regard to health or education issues, in the absence of the sort of government action that is taken for granted in developed countries. Yet these activities are not regarded as part of CSR by many Europeans, whose governments have shouldered a large element of the social responsibilities related to health, education and poverty alleviation.

Given the problem of encompassing different viewpoints in one inclusive definition of CSR, Blowfield and Frynas (2005) have proposed to think of CSR as an umbrella term for a variety of theories and practices that each recognise the following: (a) that companies have a responsibility for their impact on society and the natural environment, sometimes beyond that of legal compliance and the liability of individuals; (b) that companies have a responsibility for the behaviour of others with whom they do business (e.g., within supply chains); and (c) that business needs to manage its relationship with wider society, whether for reasons of commercial viability or to add value to society. This general definition is adopted in this book.

CSR among oil multinationals

The oil and gas sector has been among the leading industries in championing CSR. This is at least partly due to the highly visible negative effects of oil operations such as oil spills and the resulting protests by civil society groups and indigenous people. Prominent examples of publicised industry 'debacles' include oil tanker accidents such as the *Exxon Valdez*, indigenous unrest such as anti-Shell protests in Nigeria and the involvement of oil companies in human rights abuses such as BP in Colombia. Such events – widely reported by the media – have put particular pressure on multinational oil companies such as Shell and BP, which are perhaps more visible and whose brand image is more vulnerable than companies in some other sectors of the economy. The oil and gas industry appears to be under greater pressure to manage its relationship with wider society, as illustrated by the following quotation from Lord Browne, former chief executive of BP:

> Geology has not restricted the distribution of hydrocarbons to areas governed as open pluralistic democracies. The cutting edge of the issue

of corporate responsibility comes from the fact that circumstances don't always make it easy for companies to operate as they would wish. (Quoted in Levenstein and Wooding 2005, 9)

Notwithstanding the motives of the executives, oil companies pay greater lip service to CSR and they engage more with local communities than companies in many other sectors. This is demonstrated by, among other things, the remarkable growth of corporate codes of conduct and social reporting, not only among European or American firms but also the likes of Petrobras, Indian Oil and Kuwait Petroleum. Oil companies have also embraced major international initiatives such as the United Nations Global Compact and the UK government's Extractive Industries Transparency Initiative (see Chapter 2). A small number of multinational oil companies have invested in renewable energy as an alternative source of income and have pioneered climate change initiatives.

Furthermore, oil companies have initiated, funded and implemented significant community development schemes. Oil companies now help to build schools and hospitals, launch micro-credit schemes for local people and assist youth employment programmes, particularly in developing countries. They participate in partnerships with established development agencies such as the US Agency for International Development (USAID) and the United Nations Development Programme (UNDP), while using non-governmental organisations (NGOs) to implement development programmes on the ground.

Given the importance of CSR activities, the oil and gas sector is an instructive example for analysing to what extent the CSR movement can transform practices in an industry. However, the most important observation is that CSR has been adopted in the industry very unevenly. Royal Dutch Shell and BP have specifically been recognised as leaders in corporate citizenship world-wide. They spearheaded major international CSR initiatives such as the Global Compact and the Global Reporting Initiative (GRI). They have become significant players in renewable energy and have professed to combat carbon dioxide emissions in order to minimise their contribution to global warming. But other companies appear to have done less. The improvements by Shell and BP have often been contrasted with the relative lack of social and environmental engagement by Exxon – a company of a similar size to Shell and BP (Rowlands 2000; Skjærseth and Skodvin 2003).

However, Exxon has also quietly made voluntary improvements to its social and environmental performance. As Chapter 2 demonstrates, oil companies from developing countries such as Brazil's Petrobras are also initiating social and environmental programmes and have spent large sums on local community development. This suggests that the CSR movement is global in nature and that there are increased expectations of what companies are responsible for.

The analysis of oil company CSR activities in Chapter 2 suggests that the companies most engaged in CSR are companies that expand internationally and are dependent on international financial markets and international reputations. This can help to explain, for instance, the growing engagement in CSR initiatives by companies such as Brazil's Petrobras, which are increasingly operating at an international level. In contrast, CSR has not been fully embraced by companies from other developing countries, such as China and Malaysia. For instance, PetroChina continues to invest in the most repressive regimes such as those in Burma and Sudan, where the major international oil companies have long withdrawn due to human rights concerns.

One needs to remember that most of the world's oil and gas is controlled by state-owned companies from non-Western countries such as Russia, Saudi Arabia and Iran – not corporations such as Exxon and Shell. Indeed, about half of the world's known oil and gas reserves are controlled by just five national oil companies in the Middle East – Saudi Aramco, Kuwait Petroleum, the National Iranian Oil Company, Sonatrach of Algeria and the Abu Dhabi National Oil Company (Marcel and Mitchell 2005). Six out of the world's ten largest oil and gas producing companies are state-owned, and more than half of the world's fifty largest oil and gas companies are state-owned (United Nations Conference on Trade and Development 2007, 117). The oil and gas production of the state-owned companies is largely domestic; for instance, the national companies of Saudi Arabia, Iran and Mexico have no foreign production (see Table 1.2). The social and environmental records of these companies are usually under less scrutiny from civil society groups; we know, in fact, very little about their social and environmental impact. What follows is that multinational companies primarily drive the CSR agenda and we mainly focus on these companies in this book.

The aims and structure of the book

The main aim of the book is to investigate the potential of the oil and gas industry to contribute to society in its broadest sense. To put it differently, the book investigates the extent to which the development of local communities, society at large and indeed the natural environment can benefit from the voluntary activities of oil companies.

Therefore, the core chapters of the book focus on the key areas of CSR policies where oil companies are expected to make a positive contribution: improvements in environmental performance, development and governance. We want to ask to what extent the current CSR agenda can yield real improvements in these three areas.

Chapter 2 analyses the logic of CSR strategies. By providing a number of theoretical perspectives, it tries to make sense of the factors behind engaging with CSR activities. It scrutinises the CSR activities of eight oil companies around the world – ranging from Shell and BP to Indian Oil and Venezuela's PDVSA – to compare and contrast what factors pushed them to engage in CSR.

Chapter 3 provides a context for CSR in the oil and gas sector in order to set the scene for the rest of the book. It explains the basics of oil and gas production and introduces the main actors.

TABLE 1.2: *The world's largest oil and gas companies, by total production, in 2005*

Rank in world production	Company	Home country	State ownership (%)	Total production (million barrels of oil equivalent)	Foreign share of total production (%)
1	Saudi Aramco	Saudi Arabia	100	4 148.8	0
2	Gazprom	Russia	51	3 608.5	0.2
3	NIOC	Iran	100	1 810.7	0
4	Exxon	USA	0	1 725.7	82.7
5	Pemex	Mexico	100	1 666.2	0
6	BP	UK	0	1 572.6	82.1
7	Royal Dutch Shell	Netherlands/UK	0	1 482.7	70.5
8	CNPC/PetroChina	China	100	1 119.6	16.8
9	Total	France	0	997.6	75.1
10	Sonatrach	Algeria	100	911.8	0.2

Source: United Nations Conference on Trade and Development 2007, 117.

Chapters 4, 5 and 6 comprise the core of this book. These three chapters investigate the three main CSR challenges in the oil and gas sector – the environment, development and governance: Chapter 4 discusses the environmental side of CSR activities; Chapter 5 discusses company-funded development efforts; and Chapter 6 discusses governance initiatives. Each chapter starts by outlining the CSR challenge for the industry and then examines the CSR initiatives; finally, what follows is a critical assessment of the current CSR agenda.

Chapter 7 draws conclusions from the book's findings and provides some recommendations.

TWO

The logic of CSR strategies

Hundreds of academic papers have been published on CSR, but there is no consensus on how to explain the rise and direction of CSR, and there is no agreement on how CSR should be studied. The emergence of CSR has been explained as a consequence of the actions or inaction of governments and changing global governance (Jenkins 2005; Moon 2004); the spread of global communications and greater scrutiny of corporate activities by non-governmental organisations (Fabig and Boele 1999; Spar 1998); and globalisation and a changing economic environment (Korhonen 2002). However, the company responses to these global trends have been differently interpreted.

Lockett *et al.* (2006) have argued that 'the CSR field is becoming more established and distinctive, however, this does not indicate any emergence of a Kuhnian normal scientific paradigm' and that 'CSR knowledge could best be described as in a *continuing state of emergence*'. There is no accepted theoretical perspective or research methodology for making sense of CSR activities. Indeed, most scholars study CSR without any reference to a given theoretical perspective, and it has been found that CSR research is not driven by continuing scientific engagement but by 'agendas in the business environment' (Lockett *et al.* 2006).

What is particularly lacking is a general explanation as to why and how firms engage in CSR. Why do some companies display greater willingness to engage in CSR than others? Why do the same companies have different CSR policies in different countries? Why do some companies engage in CSR even if there is little external pressure to do so? In this chapter, we shall consider these issues, first by discussing different theories to explain corporate strategies and then by investigating why specific companies pursue CSR strategies.

Within the fields of management and organisation studies, the company responses to social and environmental issues have been variously explained. These theoretical perspectives include agency theory, stakeholder theory, stewardship theory, institutional theory, game theory, theory of the firm and the resource-based view in strategic management. The various theoretical perspectives are briefly summarised in Table 2.1.

While company responses to social and environmental issues have been variously explained, one can note the emergence of two dominant perspectives in the current literature. The first perspective – *stakeholder theory* – emphasises the reactions of individual firms in the context of external stakeholder relationships. This perspective can explain the different strategic responses of firms to social pressures even in the same industry or country, based on the nature of external relationships. The second perspective – *institutional theory* – emphasises the adaptation of firms to institutions in a given (for example, national or industry) context. This institutional perspective can, for instance, explain why firms from different countries or industries respond to social and environmental pressures differently and why different country subsidiaries of the same multinational firm have different CSR strategies, as a result of the prevailing national norms and beliefs.

These two perspectives can help to explain company responses to external social and environmental pressures. However, both perspectives

TABLE 2.1: *Perspectives on CSR strategies*

Theoretical perspective (alphabetical order)	Main argument	Main authors on CSR strategy
Agency theory	CSR driven by self-serving behaviour of managers at the expense of shareholders	Friedman 1962; Wright and Ferris 1997
Game theory	CSR as a trade-off between present cost and future benefits	Prasad 2005
Institutional theory	CSR driven by conformity to different institutional contexts	Doh and Guay 2006; Jennings and Zandbergen 1995
Resource-based view in strategic management	CSR can act as a specialised skill or capability to gain a competitive advantage	Hart 1995; Russo and Fouts 1997
Stakeholder theory	CSR driven by relationships with specific external actors	Clarkson 1995; Freeman 1984
Stewardship theory	CSR driven by moral imperative of managers to 'do the right thing'	Donaldson and Davis 1991
Theory of the firm	CSR driven by a supply of/demand for social activities in the marketplace	Baron 2001; McWilliams and Siegel 2001

Source: largely adapted from McWilliams *et al.* 2006.

are reactive and fail to explain active strategic choices within companies. The focus of the current literature on external stimuli fails to explain, among other things, why particular firms may use CSR as a weapon against competing firms or why specific firms may invest billions of dollars into renewable energy. Therefore, we consider a third perspective in this chapter – *Austrian economics* – which provides insights on the active pursuit of CSR strategies within companies from an entrepreneurial perspective.

This chapter investigates eight multinational oil companies to explore the applicability of the above three theoretical perspectives in explaining the social and environmental strategies of firms. We start by briefly explaining the three perspectives, and then we investigate the CSR strategies of the eight oil companies.

Stakeholders vs. institutions

Following Freeman's (1984) influential book, stakeholder theory has become the key theoretical perspective utilised within CSR debates. A stakeholder is typically defined as 'any group or individual who can affect or is affected by the achievement of the organisation's objectives' (Freeman 1984, 46). To put it differently, stakeholders are those groups that can either help or damage the firm, including employees, customers, suppliers, shareholders, banks, governments and non-governmental organisations. Freeman simply summarised the stakeholder approach as 'the principle of who or what really counts'.

Stakeholder theory predicts CSR activities as a direct result of external pressures from different actors. Typically, the relative importance of different stakeholders for the firm is considered with reference to resource or power dependence (Clarkson 1995; Freeman and Reed 1983; Jawahar and McLaughlin 2001).[1] A stakeholder is considered particularly important if: either (1) the organisation is dependent on the stakeholder for its continued survival (Freeman and Reed 1983; Jawahar and McLaughlin 2001); or (2) the stakeholder can affect the business in some way (Clarkson 1995; Freeman 1984).

Given the dominance of the stakeholder view in CSR theory and research, it is surprising that relatively few studies have empirically tested the impact of different stakeholder attributes on social and

---

[1] A number of authors have also used other criteria to assess the relative importance of stakeholders, including 'legitimacy' of a stakeholder (Hill and Jones 1992; Langtry 1994) and 'urgency' of stakeholder claims (Mitchell et al. 1997).

environmental strategies of firms (Bremmers *et al.* 2007; Olander 2007; Tsai *et al.* 2005). Therefore, it is not clear under what circumstances stakeholder theory can actually be used to explain and predict CSR strategies. At the same time, case studies show the importance of institutional contexts in determining CSR strategy (Doh and Guay 2006; Levy and Kolk 2002). Indeed, even the study on stakeholder impact by Tsai *et al.* (2005) found that the key external influence on strategy was institutional factors derived from dominant social norms, while the more traditional stakeholder attribute of resource dependence was found to be less important. The study concluded that 'a direction for future research on stakeholder influence strategies would be to combine resource dependence and institutional factors' (Tsai *et al.* 2005), which points to the importance of 'institutional theory'.

Following the influential work of writers such as Douglass North, John Meyer and Paul DiMaggio, institutional theory suggests that firms need to conform to the social norms in a given business environment because they cannot survive without a certain level of external social approval (legitimacy) (DiMaggio and Powell 1983; Meyer and Rowan 1977; North and Thomas 1973). In contrast to stakeholder theory, firms often conform not because external actors are powerful but because certain practices 'are taken for granted as "the way we do these things"' (Scott 2001, 57). Put simply, companies imitate what others do in order to remain socially acceptable.

Institutional theory predicts that firms' strategies and practices will become similar within a defined business environment, as similar firms face similar social expectations – a process known as 'institutional isomorphism'. DiMaggio and Powell (1983) identified three mechanisms through which isomorphism can occur: (1) the actions of agencies such as government regulators on which the firm is dependent (coercive isomorphism); (2) professionalisation within occupational groups with similar training, ethos and disciplinary mechanisms (normative isomorphism); and (3) executives' imitation of strategies of firms which are considered more successful or more legitimate (mimetic isomorphism).

Following institutional theory, one would expect CSR strategies to converge between firms with similar characteristics. Indeed, one Dutch study found that CSR policies are strikingly similar between Shell and BP in the oil and gas sector, Fiat and Volkswagen in the automotive sector and GlaxoSmithKline and Bristol-Myers Squibb in the pharma sector. There are also striking similarities between CSR policies in the garment industry and the food industry. As the authors concluded, 'MNCs appear only willing to state active commitment if others in their sector do as well' (Kolk and van Tulder 2006, 798). In simple terms, CSR policies become similar in a given industry because companies imitate the policies of their competitors.

Isomorphic pressures on CSR strategy have also been found as a consequence of the firms' national country of origin (Doh and Guay 2006). For instance, companies in South Africa take for granted the obligation to increase the share of black ownership (Hamann et al. 2005), while Japanese companies take for granted the importance of occupational health and safety and traditionally have very strong policies in this area compared with companies from other countries (Wokutch 1990).

While there are many differences between the stakeholder and institutional perspectives, they share important similarities. Above all, both perspectives are reactive and emphasise the role of external actors in transmitting ideas and beliefs about managerial practices to the firm. There may also be an overlap in that the same external actor may be classified both as part of the stakeholders and of the institutions; for instance, the government can be a stakeholder (e.g., as a business partner) and part of the institutional environment (e.g., creating social norms as a law maker). Table 2.2 summarises the key assumptions of both perspectives and contrasts them with the Austrian perspective discussed below.

TABLE 2.2: *Summary of theoretical perspectives on CSR strategy*

	Institutional theory	Stakeholder theory	Austrian view
Main focus	Adherence to rules and norms	Relationships with external actors	Role of the entrepreneur
Determinants of CSR strategy	Conformity to different institutional contexts	Relative dependence of a firm on stakeholders	Entrepreneurial foresight
Scope for independent managerial action	Non-choice behaviour	Limited choice behaviour	Substantial choice behaviour

Austrian economics as an alternative perspective

Recent attempts to construct a multilevel theory for explaining CSR strategies focused mainly on stakeholder theory and institutional theory and were guided by the idea that social and environmental strategies are externally driven, with the role of managers confined largely to adapting to external demands (Aguilera *et al.* 2007; Campbell 2007). However, this exclusive emphasis on adaptation to external pressures fails to allow for active managerial choices about the direction of the social and environmental strategies and does not account for entrepreneurial opportunities arising from social and environmental issues.

A number of important studies have argued that firms can obtain major business opportunities from social and environmental strategies (Mackey *et al.* 2007; Margolis and Walsh 2003; Porter and Kramer 2006), and – most crucially – that these can constitute firm-specific competitive advantages (Hart 1995; McWilliams *et al.* 2002).

Studies linking economic theory to CSR (in particular, the theory of the firm) have previously suggested that CSR can be conceived as a function of supply of/demand for social and environmental activities in the marketplace and that strategic CSR can be an integral part of a firm's differentiation strategy (Baron 2001; McWilliams and Siegel 2001). In addition, studies linking strategic management to CSR (in particular, the resource-based view) have previously suggested that specialised skills or capabilities related to investment in CSR can lead to firm-specific competitive advantages (Hart 1995; Russo and Fouts 1997). This literature implies that companies can be proactive in terms of searching for CSR-related business opportunities, in marked contrast to the reactive view presented by stakeholder theory and institutional theory.

Insights from economics and strategic management suggest that the level of CSR strategy in a firm should be viewed as an investment decision and a means towards achieving a competitive advantage, in the same manner that any other investment decisions would be taken. However, current studies with an economic or strategic focus continue to regard stakeholder relationships as the determinants of managerial decision-making and fail to consider social and environmental entrepreneurship. This book suggests therefore that we require a fresh approach to understanding active decision-making in the setting of social and environmental strategies. So-called Austrian economics can provide us with new insights.

Austrian economics was established by nineteenth- and twentieth-century economists who developed a particular line of theoretical reasoning.[2] In contrast to current approaches to CSR, Austrian economics regards human action – not external constraints – as fundamental to decision-making (Mises 1963). While this perspective stresses the importance of consumer demand as an external constraint, it suggests that human action can shape the environment

---

[2] There are a number of important distinctions between different strands of Austrian economics, which need not be recounted here (Screpanti and Zamagni 1993; Whelan 2008). The account in this chapter leans on 'rational' Austrian economics based on the work of Ludwig von Mises, which arguably presents various advantages for organisational scholarship (Whelan 2008).

too. As Mises (1940, 212) put it, 'one acts because there is change and acting itself is always change' (author's own translation from German). This line of thought is underpinned by the Austrian view that the only acceptable research propositions are those relating to individual actions and that all motivations of agents and institutions arise from individual behaviour (Mises 1963, chapter 2). By extension, entrepreneurs can choose different courses of action, and leading firms can consciously and successfully shape or change institutional structures (cf. Whelan 2008).

Furthermore, in contrast to the emphasis on *current* demand, the Austrian perspective emphasises *future* opportunities and active entrepreneurship in identifying future investments (Mises 1969; Rothbard 1962). According to this perspective, uncertainty about future market conditions is crucial and 'bestows a speculative character on entrepreneurship' (author's own translation). Uncertainty about the future leads directly to entrepreneurial profits and losses (Mises 1940, 265). The main characteristic of successful 'capitalist entrepreneurs' is thus not their ability to react to or 'discover' external demand, but rather 'their ability to make successful judgments about the future' (quoted in Whelan 2008).

The Austrian view has previously been applied to environmental economics (Cordato 2004; Faber *et al.* 1999), although no link has been made between entrepreneurial strategies and firm-specific competitive advantages. Yet a number of authors have suggested that the Austrian perspective can be readily applied to explain the strategic actions and competitive advantages at the firm level (Lewin and Phelan 1999; Roberts and Eisenhardt 2003), and the author of this book believes that it can be useful in explaining CSR strategies.

Going beyond current approaches to CSR, a firm-level Austrian perspective can explain strategic choices and outcomes on the basis of divergence of perceptions or expectations (asymmetric expectations) among economic actors, recognising that information is interpreted differently by different actors (Lewin and Phelan 1999). Indeed, one would expect CSR strategies to be driven by entrepreneurial foresight and for them to be significantly different between firms, based on divergent future expectations among decision-makers. Different interpretations of the future could explain, for instance, why some companies have been quicker than others in developing new social and environmental products, introducing policies on climate change or partnering with non-governmental organisations.

Given that a number of authors have recently pointed to the importance of entrepreneurship in CSR strategy (Baron 2007; Dixon and Clifford 2007; Spear 2006), the Austrian perspective can provide a missing link in constructing a multilevel theory of CSR strategy.

CSR strategies in the oil and gas sector

The above discussion of theoretical perspectives can help to guide us in studying to what extent CSR is driven by stakeholder demands, institutions or entrepreneurial activity. The purpose of this inquiry is not to determine which perspective is correct – each perspective can add interesting insights; rather, the purpose is to determine under what circumstances companies have acted in particular ways.

This chapter looks at CSR strategies within two different groups of companies: multinational oil companies from the UK and the United States (Shell, BP, Exxon and Chevron) and international oil companies from emerging economies (Petrobras of Brazil, Indian Oil, PDVSA of Venezuela and Kuwait Petroleum). Table 2.3 provides an overview of these eight companies.

Multinational oil companies

Shell and BP have been seen as pioneers of CSR within the oil and gas sector, and the role of stakeholders can to a large extent help to explain the birth of CSR in this sector. A series of crises led to strategic shifts in the two companies.

TABLE 2.3: *Key data on analysed oil companies*

	Headquarters	State ownership (per cent)	2006 revenues (US$ billion)	2006 profits (US$ billion)
Shell	Netherlands/ UK	0	319	25.4
BP	UK	0	274	22.0
Exxon	USA	0	347	39.5
Chevron	USA	0	201	17.1
Petrobras	Brazil	57	72	12.8
Indian Oil	India	80	45	1.7
PDVSA*	Venezuela	100	102	4.8
Kuwait Petroleum	Kuwait	100	n/a	n/a

* PDVSA figures from *Latin Business Chronicle* (25 February 2008).
Source: *Fortune* Global 500 (23 July 2007).

In 1995, Shell was attacked by Greenpeace for the planned sinking of the Brent Spar, a floating oil storage facility in the North Sea. For almost two months, the Brent Spar issue dominated media reporting in the UK and many other countries. While Greenpeace occupied the Brent Spar in the North Sea, public protests took place in many countries. Finally, in June 1995, Shell announced a reversal of its decision to sink the Brent Spar. Greenpeace claimed victory and the protests stopped (Rice and Owen 1999; Zyglidopoulos 2002). In the same year, Shell faced renewed criticism over its operations in the Ogoni area of Nigeria. For a number of years, the Ogonis (an ethnic minority of some 500,000 people) had complained about the environmental damage caused by Shell, and they demanded greater benefits from oil operations for the local people. After local protests led by the Movement for the Survival of the Ogoni People (MOSOP), Shell withdrew from the Ogoni area in 1993. But, in November 1995, the Nigerian Government executed the prominent Ogoni leader and chief Shell critic Ken Saro-Wiwa and eight others. This galvanised non-governmental organisations into supporting the Ogoni cause and new anti-Shell protests erupted around the world (Frynas 2000, 2003a).

As a result of these two crises, Shell underwent a major process of transformation. As Moody-Stuart, Chairman of the Committee of Managing Directors, wrote: 'Shell is undergoing fundamental change ... We have learned the hard way that we must listen, engage and respond to our stakeholder groups' (Frynas 2003a). In 1996, the company initiated the 'Society's Changing Expectations' project, a sophisticated audit of the views of the company's stakeholders. The Shell Group's *Statement of General Business Principles* was revised to include statements in support of fundamental human rights and sustainable development. Shell engaged in a process of dialogue with a number of stakeholders, including human rights organisations (Frynas 2003a).

BP faced stakeholder pressures in 1996 over complicity in human rights abuses in Colombia. It was revealed that the company had paid millions of dollars to the Colombian army and had provided the army with photographs and other information about anti-oil protesters, which allegedly led to intimidation, beatings and disappearances (Anonymous 1997). As one interviewee said: 'Colombia should not be overrated, but BP got the message eventually.' A senior BP manager – David Rice – admitted a number of years later:

> We've learned from our mistakes, not least because we've been challenged by NGOs. In Colombia we were accused of getting too close to the army and police in order to protect our operations. We listened, approached Human Rights Watch for advice, and then organised new security arrangements. (Rice 2002, 135)

BP initially reacted slowly to the unfolding crisis, but eventually a combination of the Colombia experience and the realisation of the rising importance of external stakeholder pressures led BP to rethink its social and environmental strategies. Like Shell, BP initiated substantial stakeholder engagement with non-governmental organisations, made public commitments on human rights and became actively involved in CSR initiatives such as the United Nations Global Compact.

Exxon's main societal crisis came in 1989 with the *Exxon Valdez* oil spill, when a tanker called *Exxon Valdez* ran aground off the coast of Alaska, spilling 11 million gallons of oil along hundreds of miles of coastline. Subsequently, Exxon spent some US$2.2 billion on clean-up costs and US$1.3 billion on legal settlements and penalties (Raeburn 1999). In addition, Exxon faced stakeholder pressures over its policy on climate change from the mid-1990s. However, the company challenged the scientific findings of environmental groups that criticised the company (with regard to both *Exxon Valdez* and climate change) and chose to combat its critics rather than to engage with them.

With regard to Exxon's lack of engagement with stakeholders, stakeholder theory can still explain Exxon's actions. The stakeholders who criticised Exxon were simply not powerful enough. While environmental groups protested against Exxon, the American oil and gas sector was able to successfully lobby the US Government (a key stakeholder) in the 1990s and 2000s to amend its policies to the benefit of companies (e.g., the defeat of President Clinton's 1993 climate change tax proposal; the 1997 US Senate resolution against ratification of the Kyoto Treaty). Indeed, it was noted that American oil companies spent more money lobbying the State of Alaska than Alaska's Department of Environmental Conservation was given to regulate the industry in 1987 (two years before the *Exxon Valdez* spill) (quoted in Bowen and Power 1993).

Unlike the companies above, Chevron did not face a defining crisis, although the company also faced some stakeholder pressures. At the company's annual meeting in 1999, 28 per cent of shareholders supported a motion for Chevron to document greenhouse gas emissions, and this may have played a part in influencing the company's shift on climate change. However, with the support of the US Government assured on issues such as climate change, American companies had relatively little to fear from other stakeholder groups. In addition, non-governmental pressures were stronger in Europe than the United States. The 2001 boycott campaign against Exxon made little impact on the company's strategy, despite shareholder resolutions and media publicity (Gueterbock 2004). The boycott was supported mainly by European non-governmental groups and failed to make real impact in Exxon's and Chevron's home base – the United States. In contrast, BP's and Shell's CSR initiatives fitted nicely with the Dutch and the British Government support for the Kyoto Treaty, and the companies faced many powerful London-based non-governmental organisations. BP and Shell simply encountered a much more powerful combination of stakeholders, including the government and non-governmental organisations.

In all four cases, therefore, the stakeholder perspective can explain major strategic change (BP and Shell) or the absence of strategic change (Exxon and Chevron). Having said this, Exxon and Chevron have engaged in CSR over time, and this cannot be explained by the stakeholder perspective. Indeed, despite the popular rhetoric about Exxon's seeming corporate irresponsibility, the steps taken by all of the oil majors towards CSR are surprisingly similar today. All four companies – Shell, BP, Exxon and Chevron – support policies such as CO_2 emission reductions, community development projects and transparency of revenues paid to governments. All four companies support broad initiatives such as the Voluntary Principles on Security and Human Rights and the Extractive Industries Transparency Initiative (see Table 2.4). Indeed, one former senior oil company executive suggested to the author that Shell and BP have been simply much better at public relations and there is not that much difference between Shell, BP or Exxon with regard to CSR; he stated: 'Exxon is a Southern Baptist company, what you see is what you get.'

TABLE 2.4: *Summary of CSR policies and initiatives by company*

| | CSR policies | | | CSR multi-stakeholder initiatives | | | |
	Reductions in CO_2 emissions	Community development projects	Government revenue transparency	United Nations Global Compact	Voluntary Principles on Security and Human Rights	Extractive Industries Transparency Initiative	World Business Council for Sustainable Development
Shell	YES	YES	YES	YES	YES	YES	YES
BP	YES	YES	YES	YES	YES	YES	YES
Exxon	YES	YES	YES	NO	YES	YES	NO
Chevron	YES	YES	YES	NO	YES	YES	YES
Petrobras	YES	YES	YES	YES	NO	NO	YES
Indian Oil	NO	YES	NO	YES	NO	NO	NO
PDVSA	NO	YES	NO	NO	NO	NO	NO
Kuwait Petroleum	NO	YES	NO	NO	NO	NO	NO

The similarity between the different oil companies can be explained through isomorphic pressures – the different companies have imitated each other, and their CSR policies have become more similar over time. Levy and Kolk (2002) have predicted that initially companies are influenced by diverse local institutional pressures, as the local context influences a company's reactions towards emerging social and environmental issues. Later on, a better understanding of the social and environmental issues and mechanisms for dealing with these issues become institutionalised within an industry. In other words, companies initially react to the pressures in their home country, but eventually common CSR tools and approaches become established within an industry.

This line of thought can, for instance, explain why initially the corporate reactions to climate change were very different between American and European companies. European companies Shell and BP accepted the inevitability of the Kyoto Treaty and worked to shape the climate change agenda. American companies Exxon and Chevron denied the validity of scientific evidence on climate change and opposed any mandatory reductions in CO_2 emissions (Rowlands 2000; Skjærseth and Skodvin 2003). National institutions can also explain different reactions by different subsidiaries of the same company. Levy and Kolk (2002) noted that Shell Europe had accepted the need for international emissions controls in the mid-1990s, while Shell US was still a member of the Global Climate Coalition (GCC), a corporate lobby group which spent tens of millions of dollars trying to undermine the international climate negotiations.

Levy and Kolk's (2002) line of thought can also explain why the policies of the different oil companies have converged over time. Taking climate change strategies as an example of this convergence, they argued:

> Participation in industry associations and climate change meetings provided arenas within which expectations concerning science, policy, markets and technologies tended to converge. Key managers

> responsible for climate strategy in each of the companies studied were on first name terms and had met each other frequently during many official negotiating sessions and conferences. European companies have participated in the American Petroleum Institute and the GCC, while American companies attend European industry meetings. (Levy and Kolk 2002, 294)

Interactions of this type within an industry can help to explain the dissemination of ideas on how to deal with a given social and environmental issue. Michael Marvin, the director of the Business Council for Sustainable Energy, stated that 'companies don't come [to our meetings] expecting to change their positions, but they move by a process of osmosis' (quoted in Levy and Kolk 2002, 295). Therefore, while the CEOs of Exxon – Lee Raymond (1993–2005) and Rex Tillerson (CEO from 2006) – never fully embraced CSR, even Exxon have come to accept the need for precautionary action and the adoption of a range of CSR policies, which were increasingly viewed as an industry standard. The company has moved from a position of not even acknowledging the existence of global warming towards discussing the merits of a carbon-cap-and-trade system versus a carbon tax and engaging with critics, including environmentalists and religious groups (Colvin 2007).

None the less, while institutional pressures are clearly at work, the strategies of the major oil companies are far from identical. As one example, neither Exxon nor Chevron has joined the United Nations Global Compact (see Table 2.4). While Shell and BP have invested billions of dollars in renewable energy such as wind and solar, Exxon has chosen to keep away from wind and solar energy and has invested in new technology for reducing CO_2 emissions from hydrocarbons; Exxon has also partnered up with the automotive industry to render car engines more efficient. Somewhere in between these two strategies, Chevron has invested in hydrogen fuel cell technology and batteries for hybrid cars. According to interviewees, the reason for these differences was, to a certain extent, different interpretations of future markets.

In the late 1990s, Shell and BP envisaged large markets for renewable energy in the future. The creation of Shell International Renewables in November 1997 was reportedly based on Shell's optimistic expectation that renewable energy will supply 5–10 per cent of the world's energy needs by 2020, which could perhaps rise to more than 50 per cent by mid-century (Knott 1999). In contrast, Exxon experts dismissed the potential for renewable energy, based on their own forecast that renewable energy will only reduce petrol consumption by no more than 5 per cent by 2020. As one Exxon interviewee put it bluntly: 'We will run on gas in twenty years, you can't change that.' In the case of Exxon – as in the case of BP and Shell – the decision to invest or not invest in renewable energy was driven by entrepreneurial foresight.

In the case of Exxon, its anticipation of future markets was additionally influenced by its individual entrepreneurial experience. In the wake of the 1970s oil crises, the company made significant investment in solar energy research, and it reportedly still holds dozens of patents in the solar energy field. However, the programme was discontinued on account of the lack of profitability (Colvin 2007), so new investment in renewable energy would seem an unwise entrepreneurial choice to many Exxon managers.

There is also evidence that oil majors have used CSR strategies to enter new markets or to protect existing ones. Frynas (2005) has found that social investments can provide companies with competitive advantages vis-à-vis other companies with less social engagement. This is all the more important today, since the oil majors have only restricted access to many of the world's oil reserves. Access to Saudi Arabian oil reserves is restricted, and partial nationalisations in Venezuela and Russia in recent years have heightened uncertainty among Western companies, while increasing competition from oil companies from emerging markets such as China, India, Brazil and Malaysia has further limited access to oil resources for Western companies.

In a number of oil-producing countries, socially responsive oil companies appear to have been favoured by the government in the award of oil and gas concessions. For instance, Chevron in Angola appears to have strategically used its social investments in its bid to renew its stake in Block 0, Angola's most prized oil asset (see Chapter 5 for more details). The Chevron-Angola example demonstrates that corporate expertise in managing social and environmental issues can be used as a proactive weapon in global competition.

Oil companies from emerging economies

The CSR strategies of oil companies from emerging economies are far less well-documented than those by Shell or Exxon, so it is more difficult to trace their evolution. The strategies of these companies are also likely to be different because they are fully or partially government-owned. Kuwait Petroleum and Venezuela's PDVSA are 100 per cent government-owned. The Indian government holds just over 80 per cent of Indian Oil shares, while the Brazilian Government controls 57 per cent of the voting shares of Petrobras.

Given that the government is the key shareholder/stakeholder in all of the four companies, it can use the companies to advance its own agenda, sometimes at the expense of minority shareholders. Indeed, many of the social and environmental strategies of the four companies can be explained as a result of government policy. This can help to explain the oil companies' emphasis on contributions to the local social and economic development. To a varying extent, all four companies have been expected to contribute towards national infrastructure development, including road and hospital construction, agricultural initiatives, and skills development. Indeed, local community development (or philanthropy in Western terms) is considered the central part of social responsibility for Indian Oil, PDVSA and Petrobras.

Indeed, the government influenced the very meaning of 'socially responsible' in respective countries. From its inception, Kuwait

Petroleum was expected to help in the development of the country's infrastructure as part of its responsibilities; however, over time the government took on many of its previous infrastructure responsibilities and redefined the company's primary social responsibility as driving economic growth and employing local staff. In Venezuela, the government did the opposite. Before 2002, PDVSA was largely seen as a commercial entity with the primary responsibility of generating economic benefits for the country. President Chavez redefined the social responsibilities of PDVSA from 2002 and (in the words of one interviewee) 'turned PDVSA into a social change agent'. Accordingly, the influence of government can explain the fact that 'the social strategies of PDVSA after 2002 have been idiosyncratic by international standards' (in the words of one interviewee); for instance, PDVSA helped to establish and fund rural co-operatives (a Marxist-influenced idea).

Similarly in Brazil, Petrobras pursued certain social and environmental strategies as a result of government pressures. For instance, Petrobras previously made investments in thermoelectric projects as a result of the Brazilian Government's plans in 2000–1; the projects turned out to be loss making, and the company then attempted to reduce its investments over the course of several years.

In all of these cases, stakeholder pressure (the government) can explain the companies' social and environmental strategies. Government pressure can also explain the big differences between the social and environmental strategies in the different companies – after all, the different governments have very different agendas. In summary, stakeholder theory can explain many of the social and environmental strategies of state-owned companies.

However, there is evidence that stakeholder pressures from the government have become less important for the different state-owned companies over time, except for PDVSA. Most notably, Indian Oil has undergone a major transformation over the last decade or so; in the 1970s, the Indian government specified a twenty-point economic programme (including such goals as provision of drinking water and rural electrification), and Indian companies were evaluated against these goals (Prasad 2005), whereas today Indian Oil has a large measure of autonomy from the government in setting its social and environmental goals.

At the same time, the stakeholder perspective still fails to explain why specific state-owned firms have pursued certain CSR strategies in the absence of stakeholder pressures. In 2006, Kuwait Petroleum hired the UK-based Institute of Business Ethics to design an ethical policy for the company, including a code of conduct – despite the fact that the company faced little external pressure to do so. Before 2002, PDVSA had started to develop Western-style social and environmental strategies and even won a CSR award in Brazil in 2002, despite the fact that it faced no pressure from the Venezuelan Government or the weak Venezuelan civil society to do so. Indeed, stakeholder pressures cannot explain why PDVSA started to develop CSR policies in the first instance.

Interview data suggests that interactions with Western partners were behind the drive to adopt Western-style approaches. Leadership from the top can provide part of the explanation; for instance, one interviewee said with reference to Kuwait Petroleum's ethical policy that 'the sheikh thought this was important'. However, international exposure appears to have been crucial either in persuading the Kuwaiti decision-makers or Luis Justi – the former managing director of PDVSA – that the companies should have a Western-style social and environmental strategy. Interviewees suggested that the adoption of Western CSR tools could be explained on the basis of 'international credibility', 'interacting with Western oil executives', 'joint ventures' or simply 'part of the trend and expectations'.

Kuwait Petroleum and PDVSA have pursued international expansion for a long time, and – unlike many other national oil companies – they have extensive foreign oil and gas investments and marketing operations in developed countries. Kuwait Petroleum's drive to become a global company started as early as in 1981 with a US$2.56 billion agreement to purchase the US company Santa Fe International (Tétreault 1995, 32–41), while PDVSA started a series of international ventures from the mid-1980s, notably the acquisition of the US company Citco (Baena 1999). International joint ventures appear to have been important mechanisms for transmitting international practices, acting as isomorphic pressures. Kuwait Petroleum partnered up with Shell and BP to explore investment opportunities in Asia, while PDVSA engaged in partnerships with multinational companies such as Shell before 2002. The international expansion plans of Petrobras and Indian Oil were less ambitious. Petrobras considers itself more a regional company in Latin America rather than a global company, having become the second-largest energy company in Bolivia and Argentina. Indian Oil has opened offices in Kuwait, Dubai and Malaysia, and its international expansion has a regional focus on Asia and developing economies, including Trinidad and Tobago. None the less, both companies have collaborated with various international firms and have been exposed to international markets and, by extension, to some of the same institutional pressures as other international companies.

Institutional pressures can help to explain why diverse companies such as Kuwait Petroleum, PDVSA (pre-2002) and Indian Oil have begun to pay more attention to environmental issues, which were previously neglected. For example, PDVSA started a development agreement with Shell and Mitsubishi in around 2000, which in turn created a 'sustainable development' team to study the potential social and environmental impacts of a planned project; the team was able to introduce new ideas about sustainability into PDVSA. Similarly, institutional pressures can explain why both Petrobras and Indian Oil decided to join the United Nations Global Compact (see Table 2.4). A Petrobras interviewee commented: 'This [Global Compact membership] shows that we are now global.' Indeed,

Petrobras won an international CSR award in 2006 for a farming project which explicitly adopted the United Nations Millennium Development Goals.

None the less, oil companies from emerging economies did not, by and large, conceive of social and environmental strategies as business opportunities, unlike Shell or BP. For instance, Petrobras's thermoelectric projects were driven by Brazilian Government pressures, while Kuwait Petroleum's environmental improvements across its refineries were driven by European environmental regulations, which imposed quality standards for petroleum products in the European Union. These reluctant investments were a passive reaction to changes in the external business environment, not entrepreneurial initiatives.

Indeed, in contrast to the American and British multinational oil companies, there is little evidence of long-term planning in terms of social and environmental issues, and CSR appears to be generally less of a strategic tool. The most notable exception was Kuwait Petroleum's introduction of unleaded petrol in the European market in 1984, following a policy announcement of a plan to provide tax breaks for unleaded petrol within the European Community. In the same year, Kuwait Petroleum International launched 'unleaded petrol' accompanied by a large publicity campaign in order to obtain a first mover advantage ahead of companies such as Shell. Ralph Brown, the company's marketing director, reportedly said: 'since we were going to have to do it anyway in the near future, we might as well do it on our own timing' (Tétreault 1995, 63). This was an early example of an entrepreneurial green initiative by a national oil company. However, the initiative did not form part of a longer-term strategic plan, and Kuwait Petroleum managers' entrepreneurial initiatives within the company were stifled in later years by state policy and bureaucracy, which ultimately limits entrepreneurial potential in all state-owned national oil companies.

Conclusions on CSR strategies

The above analysis of oil companies suggests that all three perspectives – stakeholder theory, institutional theory and Austrian economics – have a part to play in explaining the social and environmental strategies of multinational companies. However, it appears that the explanatory strength of a particular perspective varies between companies and over time.

Stakeholder government pressures have played a key role in influencing the social and environmental strategies of state-owned companies. Pressures from non-governmental organisations also appear to have initially played an important part in shaping corporate strategies for Shell and BP. None the less, institutional pressures and isomorphism appear to have become more dominant over time. To put it differently, stakeholders can trigger a radical change in company strategy initially; once CSR tools and practices become more sophisticated and developed, they spread across an industry via professional meetings, memberships of the same associations and joint ventures, and then become accepted norms.

This pattern seems to support previous research on social and environmental strategies, which suggested that the local context gives way to convergence pressures over time (Levy and Kolk 2002) and supports the previous insight that social and environmental movements can give rise to widely accepted institutional structures within an industry (Lounsbury et al. 2003). Therefore, stakeholder pressures become less important over time. Stakeholder pressures are still important for state-owned companies where the government-owner continues to play a central role, but convergence pressures can also be seen within state-owned companies. The CSR policies of Kuwait Petroleum, Petrobras or pre-2002 PDVSA have clearly been influenced by interactions with other firms in international markets.

While stakeholder and institutional pressures continue to be important, this research strongly suggests that CSR strategy is not merely a reaction to external pressures. Rather, companies use CSR in order to gain competitive advantages in terms of obtaining preferential treatment by governments or in terms of entering new markets. Active entrepreneurship plays a role in formulating social and environmental strategies. Shell's and BP's investment in renewable energy cannot be explained through either external pressures or a theory of the firm/the resource-based perspective. A company does not invest a billion dollars in order to react to external pressures or current demand alone. Likewise, the market did not communicate to Shell and BP an urgent need to invest in renewable energy, nor did these firms have unique capabilities to pursue a renewable energy strategy. Yet this type of investment can be readily explained from the Austrian perspective, which assumes that the key characteristic of a successful entrepreneur is the ability to make successful judgments about the future (Mises 1969; Rothbard 1962). Following the Austrian idea of 'entrepreneurial foresight', companies have made different assumptions about the future with regard to the future importance of ethical concerns, the finite nature of oil and gas reserves or the commercial viability of renewable energies in ten years. These assumptions necessarily shape future social and environmental strategies because companies need to reconcile any 'ethical' considerations with commercial considerations.

There is little evidence that companies from emerging economies have pursued entrepreneurial opportunities with regard to CSR. Even when companies such as PDVSA and Kuwait Petroleum faced global competitive pressures and were exposed to international markets, 'green' entrepreneurial activity was limited. In contrast, Western multinational companies face strong competitive pressures, are driven purely by commercial concerns and their access to many of the world's oil reserves is limited, so they need to use any available means to gain a competitive advantage over their rivals. CSR may just be one of those means.

In conclusion, we require a multilevel theoretical perspective to explain the social and environmental strategies of companies. This research merely provides a starting point, and our conclusions have to be tentative at this stage, but it points to the importance of institutional pressures and entrepreneurship in shaping corporate strategy. It is clear that the stakeholder perspective – which has been most frequently used to explain CSR – is insufficient. The evolution of CSR is a complex process.

THREE

The context of CSR

Discussions on CSR often revolve around attempts to find 'universal' solutions that can be uniformly applied across the world. Ethical codes and principles such as the United Nations Global Compact, certification schemes such as the ISO 14001 or standards for reporting such as the Global Reporting Initiative attempt to universalise social and environmental standards. There are good arguments for applying the same universal standards: certain standards are becoming a legal requirement, unambiguous criteria simplify the work of managers and auditors and universal standards increase transparency in information flows about corporate conduct around the world (Paine *et al.* 2005; Smeltzer and Jennings 2006).

However, there are major problems with applying the same rules and practices everywhere. Indeed, the crucial challenge is to explore the potential and limitations of CSR in specific settings, because the success of CSR initiatives is highly dependent on the context. The same initiative may be appropriate in one country but not elsewhere; it may work in one sector but not in other sectors; it may be successful in one situation but not on other occasions. The universal assumptions about the social and political conditions for the success of CSR initiatives are also unrealistic, as we explore further in Chapter 6.

Previous research has clearly demonstrated the limits of universal standards. First, universal CSR standards fail to address specific national contexts. Examples include corporate initiatives on black empowerment and HIV/Aids to tackle the legacy of the apartheid in South Africa (Hamann *et al.* 2005), initiatives to deal with the effects of the economic crisis in Argentina (Newell and Muro 2006), or specific women's labour issues in Islamic countries such as 'menstruation leave' in Indonesia (Frynas 2003b). Second, universal CSR standards are capable of addressing some issues better than others. For instance, universal codes of conduct can improve basic working conditions in some instances, but they are less able to tackle patterns of discrimination and harassment in the workplace (Jenkins *et al.* 2002).

Finally, the nature of an industry determines CSR concerns, and social concerns are highly diverse between different industries. For instance, the clothing industry raises issues of employment conditions and the responsibility of firms within complex global supply chains (Frynas 2003b), fast food restaurants raise the issue of obesity (Adams 2005), while the main issue in the tobacco industry is the long-term health effects of smoking (Palazzo and Richter 2005). These concerns may vary between countries, but the key concerns related to an industry's operations are typically shared in most countries. Nigeria is very different from Azerbaijan, but some of the key concerns related to the oil and gas sector are very similar in both countries – the environmental impact (such as oil spills), the social impact of oil operations on local communities and macro-economic difficulties created by the inflow of oil revenues. That is why it is always crucial to understand the industry context within which CSR operates. This chapter is devoted to investigating the industry context.

The following sections aim to explain the oil and gas industry and its wider impact in simple terms. By the end of this chapter, the reader should have a much better idea of how the oil business works and what social, environmental and economic issues oil operations raise.

The product

The nature of products and services necessarily determines CSR concerns, so we start by explaining the nature of crude oil. Crude oil (or petroleum) is a hydrocarbon material of ancient animal and vegetable origin. The word hydrocarbon refers to mixtures of chemical substances, which primarily consist of carbon and hydrogen atoms. But names can be confusing to the layman. As liquid and gaseous hydrocarbons are closely related, the word 'petroleum' is sometimes used to refer to both petroleum and natural gas. Coal is also a hydrocarbon, but petroleum-related books usually refer to oil and natural gas when they talk about hydrocarbons.

Hydrocarbons come in different shapes and have very different characteristics. The popular image of crude oil is as a liquid black or brown substance, but crude oils can also be pale yellow or green. Crude oils also vary in many other respects: they can be runny liquids or thick and sticky, they can have a 'high' or 'low' sulphur content, etc. The most common way to classify different crude oils is °API gravity, which stands for the American Petroleum Institute standard. Every crude oil has a different gravity, which usually ranges from about 20 to 40° API. Lighter (less dense) oils have high °API gravity and are more sought after (Stoneley 1995, 29). Furthermore, crude oil from each oilfield is unique. The characteristics of a specific crude oil type influence the commercial value of the oil. For instance, many West African varieties such as Nigeria's Bonny Light have a higher value than, say, Mexico's Maya, as they have a higher °API gravity and lower sulphur content.[1]

---

[1] Refineries usually prefer crude oil with a low sulphur content because they must remove the sulphur from the oil (Hyne 1995, 14). However, the characteristics of crude oil from the same oil field can also change slightly over time. This presents problems for both the handling of oil by refineries and the determination of the sale price.

Petrol for cars or wax for candles can come from the same crude oil. Through processing, crude oil can be converted into, among other things, gasoline, kerosene, lubricating oil, fuel oil, asphalt and paraffin. Oil refineries process and separate the different hydrocarbons and also break down some of the heavy ones into lighter and more commercially 'useful' products. Since crude oil is of little use by itself, the commercial value of a specific crude oil depends on the proportion of 'useful' products that it can yield; for instance, light oil yields proportionately more gasoline than heavy oil.

When oil is produced, natural gas is often found in the same oil reservoir and it flows to the surface in an oil/gas/water mixture – this is called 'associated gas'. Only several decades ago, natural gas was not of much interest to oil companies. In the middle of the twentieth century, when gas was found on its own, the find was sometimes classified as 'dry' (that means, a drilling which did not result in any significant findings). This has changed considerably since then, with some developing nations such as Algeria and Indonesia having become important gas exporting nations. As natural gas may occur on its own (i.e., without the presence of oil – this is called 'non-associated gas'), many gas fields are developed specifically for gas production today. Major oil companies such as Shell are just as important gas producers as they are oil producers; when we talk about the oil industry, we usually mean both oil and gas.

As with crude oil, gaseous hydrocarbons have different characteristics and their commercial value varies. Gas is classified as 'wet' or 'dry', 'sour' or 'sweet'. As with crude oil, low sulphur content is advantageous in gas. The terms 'sour' and 'sweet' refer to the sulphur content in oil or gas; a 'sweet gas' contains little or no sulphur (the same applies to the term 'sweet crude oil'). The terms 'wet' and 'dry' refer to the content of hydrocarbons which can be recovered from gas as liquid products. Natural gas can contain various hydrocarbons which can be extracted as liquids during processing; gas with significant amounts of such hydrocarbons is called 'wet'.[2]

The above description of the product indicates that hydrocarbons are very complex products for the layman to understand, unlike garments or commodities such as coffee. This is particularly relevant to developing countries, where local people exposed to the industry's activities have often not fully understood the complexity and the impact of oil and gas operations. Previous fieldwork by the author suggests that local people in developing economies have blamed oil companies – sometimes unfairly – for the effects of oil spills, gas flaring and dust created by lorries, yet they sometimes failed to link oil activities to effects such as changing fish stock levels or certain health difficulties. The effects of oil operations can be difficult to measure and document, and even courts have found it difficult to attribute causality between oil activities and adverse effects on the local people (Frynas 2000, 181). Crude oil and natural gas are also less visible for the end-consumer because they are processed to yield other products ranging from plastics to construction materials. A holistic understanding of the industry's social and environmental impact depends, therefore, on a relatively high level of technical expertise.

The industry's social and environmental impact does, of course, depend on the manner in which companies operate. The next section explains how companies go about finding and producing hydrocarbons.

Exploration and production

In the early days of the modern oil and gas industry in the nineteenth century, the search for oil was conducted in a haphazard manner. Oil

---

[2] Wet gas is usually associated with oil, while dry gas is usually non-associated and contains a high proportion of methane, a simple and light gaseous hydrocarbon. Wet gas can be commercially valuable because of the liquid products it can yield.

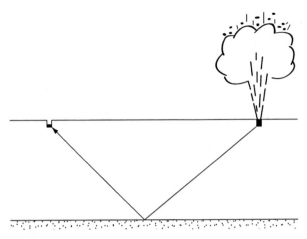

Figure 3.1: Seismic survey

wells were drilled where oil seeped to the surface by itself or wells were drilled on 'instinct', and only occasionally might the oil company employ a geologist. Today, the oil and gas industry requires cutting-edge technical skills, ranging from satellite technology to 3D computer imaging, and oil companies employ whole armies of petroleum engineers and very specialised smaller subcontracting firms.

Even before oil production takes place, oil operations already require substantial investment and substantial interactions with the government and local communities during exploration for oil. Exploration requires so-called seismic surveys and exploration drilling. In a seismic survey, sound waves are sent into the earth's crust, where they are reflected by the different rock layers. The sound energy from a source on the surface bounces off the different rock layers and returns to the surface, where it is recorded by a detector (see Figure 3.1). Surveys are carried out by seismic crews, which are usually subcontractors of oil companies and can include hundreds of men. The seismic crew measures the time taken for the wave to return to the surface, which reveals the depth of the layers and also indicates what types of rock lie beneath the surface (Hyne 1995). In the sea and in riverine areas seismic surveys are carried out using boats equipped

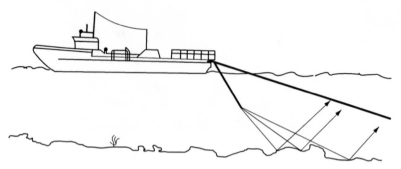

Figure 3.2: Seismic method at sea and in riverine areas

with air guns which release compressed air (instead of explosives used in onshore areas) into the water surface. The equipment is towed in the water behind the boat (see Figure 3.2).

Following seismic surveys, drilling of exploration wells begins in areas where oil reserves are suspected. This may already involve the construction of some infrastructure, as vegetation may need to be cleared and access roads to the well site may need to be built (this does not apply to drilling in the sea). Wells are drilled with rotary cutting tools with tough metal or diamond teeth that can bore through the hardest rock. These tools are suspended on a drilling string. During drilling operations, information about the oilfield at various depths is collected by examining drill cuttings, which are returned to the surface. Drilling is the only way to exactly determine whether there is oil under the surface and to estimate its amount, although drilling costs can be very high, which puts a limit on the number of drilling sites. If there is no oil in commercial quantities, this so-called 'dry hole' is plugged and abandoned. If oil is discovered in the exploration well, so-called 'appraisal wells' are drilled in the area in order to establish the size of the field. If the field is to be commercially exploited, some of these appraisal wells may later be used as so-called 'development wells' for oil production (Hyne 1995).

Once the production stage starts, an oil/gas/water mixture flows to the surface. Oil companies cannot pump oil alone, because gas and

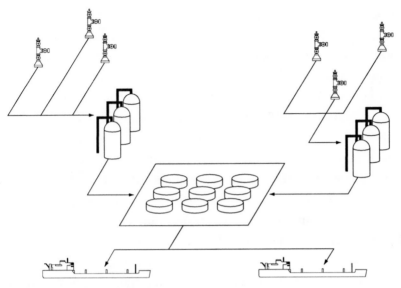

Figure 3.3: Typical oil production activities

water are located in a petroleum trap together with the oil. Gas flows to the surface by itself because it is very light. Oil can sometimes flow to the surface by itself if there is enough 'pressure' in the reservoir, but oil is more commonly brought to the surface artificially by pumps or other methods. Once the natural reservoir drive has finished, water is injected into the earth's crust to force some of the remaining oil to flow to the surface (Hyne 1995).

From the surface, the oil/gas/water mixture is transported through a pipe to a gathering station called a flowstation, where gas and liquids are separated. The oil is then either (1) transported through a pipeline directly to a local refinery; or (2) exported through a pipeline to a foreign refinery (e.g., pipelines from Algeria and Libya to Western Europe); or (3) – as is common in most developing economies – transported to an export terminal on the coast where the crude oil is loaded on to tankers and shipped abroad (see Figure 3.3). The basics of oil production in offshore areas are not very different, but the production techniques can be much more technologically sophisticated. In deep water areas, oil companies no longer use fixed oil platforms tied to the seabed; instead, they use huge ships, which float on the water far above the oilfield. These ships or vessels are used to separate the oil/gas/water mixture and to store the oil until a tanker arrives to take the crude oil away. The ship is connected to the ocean surface through various cables and the drilling equipment. Oil companies use underwater GPS-style satellite systems, which can pinpoint the location of drilling equipment to the centimetre; and all of this drilling activity happens at a distance of many hundreds of metres or several kilometres below the ship.

The above outline of the industry's production processes reveals a highly technical industry, using highly sophisticated technology and equipment. At the same time, the industry has a high potential to cause negative social and environmental effects, from the exploration phase through to the production phase, ranging from the impact of migration into rural areas during seismic studies to the impact of oil spills during production and transport (this is discussed in greater detail in Chapter 4). Indeed, the oil and gas industry cannot function without seismic surveys or infrastructure such as access roads, which requires interactions between the oil companies and the local people and carries the risk of diverse social and environmental effects, particularly in highly populated or ecologically vulnerable areas.

Marketing

CSR activities typically focus on oil exploration and production – also known as 'upstream activities'. The so-called 'downstream activities' – oil refining and the marketing of oil products, which add value to the product, tend to cause less controversy. In addition, in many developing economies, such as Nigeria and Azerbaijan, there are few domestic refineries and petrochemical industries, so the bulk of the crude oil is exported to foreign refineries in North America, Europe and Far East Asia, where the crude oil is later transformed into petrol, jet kerosene and other products.

None the less, it is useful to outline some of the complexity of oil marketing because it helps to understand the involvement of different actors in oil operations. The landscape of international oil markets has undergone major changes in the last twenty years. By the early 1980s, a so-called 'spot market' began to grow in importance and eventually replaced the previous system of fixed prices, following Saudi Arabia's decision to abandon government-determined official prices in 1985. On the most basic level, a spot market for crude oil is a market for the sale and purchase of oil for immediate delivery, in contrast to the 'futures market' which provides for delivery at some point in the future. A crude oil spot market sale is the sale of one crude oil cargo for immediate delivery at a price negotiated at the time of the agreement. Thus, traders can buy a specific cargo for immediate delivery or for future delivery.

In fact, most of the oil today is still delivered under fixed contracts between producers and refiners. However, the spot market helps to determine a realistic price of oil in the world market – based on the available supply of and demand for oil. The price of the oil is calculated using complex formulas and is usually 'benchmarked' (that is, related or compared) against the price of a leading crude oil type: the Brent crude from the North Sea, the Dubai crude or West Texas Intermediate. The price is adjusted according to the characteristics of the particular oil – a barrel of better quality oil may fetch several dollars more than a barrel of lower quality oil.

While the pricing of crude oil is now largely ruled by the market, developing economy governments still play a major role in the international oil market. During the nationalisations of the 1970s, governments of oil-producing states came to own a substantial part of the oil produced. As we pointed out in Chapter 1, about half of the world's known oil and gas reserves are controlled by just five national oil companies in the Middle East, and state-owned companies from countries such as Venezuela, Russia and Nigeria control another large part of the oil reserves. Therefore, oil sales on the world market are often negotiated by the government (via a national oil corporation), not the private oil companies. The government either sells a cargo of oil on the spot market or by using a so-called 'term contract'. Unlike a spot sale, where a single cargo is sold, a term contract usually involves multiple deliveries of oil to a specific buyer for a fixed time period at an agreed price formula (but the price is usually linked to the spot prices of the specified benchmark crude oil).

While governments tend to sell their crude oil on the world market (with a few exceptions, such as Kuwait Petroleum with its international network of petrol stations), larger integrated oil companies such as Shell or Exxon often use their crude oil within their own company (although they also sell and buy crude oil on the spot market). As a result of these complex trade relationships, oil from the same oilfield may end up in different hands in various parts of the world. For instance, Angolan oil is sold both on the spot market and through the use of 'term contracts' with regular buyers including oil refineries on the east coast of the United States (such as Sun Oil), oil traders (such as Glencore of Switzerland) and multinational oil companies (such as Chevron). The buyers may, in turn, resell the oil to others. Indeed, an oil cargo sold at a loading terminal in a developing economy may change ownership many times before it reaches the oil refinery. The marketing of natural gas is similar to that of oil, but the sale of natural gas tends to rely to a much larger extent on long-term contracts than spot contracts.

As the above account shows, marketing operations in the oil and gas sector raise the issue of the degree of involvement of different actors along the global supply chain, which in turn raises questions over the degree of responsibility of a particular company for the social and environmental impact of oil operations. The global integration of production, where one company (e.g., Shell or Exxon) controls all of the stages of the supply chain – starting with production of crude oil and ending with marketing petroleum products to the end-consumer – is not the norm. The host governments and the companies that produce crude oil on their behalf have a lot of power over the supply and the pricing of the product, often far exceeding that of the buyer in the petrochemical sector. State-owned companies control a significant part of the global supply of crude oil, while 'middlemen' such as trading companies may also be involved. Therefore, in contrast to 'buyer-driven' global supply chains that exist in the clothing industry or the food industry (Barrientos and Smith 2007; Tallontire 2007), the attribution of social responsibility for 'upstream oil activities' to a buyer (e.g., a refiner such as Sun Oil) is often not possible.

The complex relationships in the oil and gas sector also raise the question of the responsibility of a range of actors other than oil companies. It is useful to summarise who these key stakeholders are, which we shall do in the next section.

Stakeholders

Multinational oil companies such as Shell could not operate successfully without the involvement of other stakeholders, who provide the legal guarantees, funding, equipment, technical expertise for oil operations and legitimacy. The web of relationships of an oil company is very complex. As an example, Figure 3.4 provides a typology of the stakeholder groups of Shell International – the Shell company's London-based hub. Behind each of the headings, there may be numerous organisations with sometimes very different interests. Figure 3.4 does not even include stakeholders involved in operational activities in developing economies; Shell's subsidiaries in different parts of the world will have many other stakeholder groups. For instance, the stakeholders of Shell's oil-producing subsidiary will also include international subcontracting firms such as Schlumberger and Wilbros, local firms, local communities represented by different organisations and persons, different government agencies and so on. It may be useful to sketch out

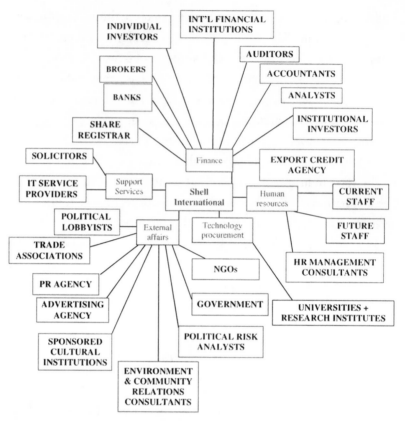

Figure 3.4: Stakeholders of Shell International
Source: adapted from Platform Website at www.carbonweb.org/
Reproduced with permission of Platform.

the importance of a number of key stakeholders/actors and the respective roles they play in CSR policies (see Table 3.1 for a summary).

The government

Work by institutional theorists reminds us that, despite globalisation, nation-states remain the primary units of political competition and mobilisation, national legal systems continue to standardise the nature of property rights in an economy and national regulations continue to

TABLE 3.1: *Key stakeholder groups in the oil and gas sector and their interest in CSR*

	Interest in supporting CSR	Limitations
Government	– Gain aid from donors – Avoid the need for government intervention	– Lack of capacity to support social and environmental initiatives – Corruption
Financial Institutions	– Protect own reputation – Maintain operations of companies in host countries	– Social benefits secondary to profits – Limited power to influence oil-producing countries
Contractors	– Improved relationships with local communities – Continued business relationship with the oil company	– Less concern with external reputation – Small volume of trade with a specific client oil company
NGOs	– Pursue shared goals with the business community – Secure funding – Influence emerging CSR standards, codes and 'social norms'	– Lack of accountability – Ineffective at providing services

govern industry entry and exit and many other aspects of market activity (Whitley 1999). Even in the most dysfunctional African states, with weak government authority, the state continues to exert an important influence on the country's development (Wood and Frynas 2006).

Accordingly, the crucial partner for an oil company is the government, and this is particularly relevant in the oil and gas sector. In most countries of the world, oil resources are vested in the state, and the government decides which company gets access to the country's natural resources through the granting of oil licences. The government also provides the regulatory framework, such as petroleum tax and royalty, and defines the respective rights and responsibilities of investors and the communities that host them through property rights, planning rules and systems of redress. Since the oil and gas sector is considered 'strategic' in many developing economies, the government sometimes imposes minimum drilling obligations, price controls, control over the development of oilfields (including restrictions on production) and, in some cases, can expropriate the assets of oil companies or cancel contracts. Political decisions directly influence the day-to-day operations of the oil and gas industry, particularly if the state has a shareholding interest in a company.

Furthermore, there is a direct relationship between state welfare provision and the need for CSR initiatives. Multinational oil companies have generally been asked to voluntarily take on greater social and environmental responsibilities in countries where the government has not been successful in providing public goods and effective regulation. For example, oil companies in Nigeria have been pressured to build schools and hospitals, because the state has failed to provide those public goods for the local communities in Nigeria's oil-producing areas (Frynas 2001, 2005). In other oil-producing countries such as Saudi Arabia and Kuwait, oil companies face less pressure to fulfil such roles in large measure because the state has gradually become more effective in providing public goods (Marcel and Mitchell 2005, chapter 6). When asked about local community projects in Egypt, an oil company manager responded: 'we give some charitable donations, but the government takes care of things', which means that there is relatively little pressure on companies to engage in social investment.

In general, the effectiveness of government (as well as stakeholder pressure) can help to explain why companies devote more resources to CSR in some countries rather than others. For instance, BP spent millions on social initiatives and CSR in Angola; however, a former BP manager pointed out the contrast with other countries: 'BP is the greatest investor in Algeria but nothing is done on CSR.' Likewise, if the government is able to effectively enforce high environmental standards in an industry, there is no need for companies to voluntarily embark on environmental activities. To put it differently, if the government 'takes care' of its citizens, there is relatively little need for CSR.

As a result, the very concept of CSR depends on the role of government. In a country such as Nigeria, where the government has failed to effectively enforce environmental regulation, a company's care to avoid oil spills can be considered voluntary and can be labelled 'CSR'. In a country such as Norway, where the government has effectively enforced high environmental standards in the industry, a company's care to avoid oil spills can be arguably labelled 'regulatory compliance'. Of course, a company such as Statoil may act responsibly anyway, and it may be partly motivated by social responsibility when it avoids oil spills in Norway. However, the role of the government remains crucial in determining what activities can be considered 'voluntary' and 'beyond legal compliance' (the characteristics of a CSR definition).

It has also been shown that the effectiveness of some CSR strategies in the oil and gas sector depends on government support (Frynas 2005; Gulbrandsen and Moe 2007). Chapters 5 and 6 in this book illustrate that the effective delivery of local community development projects and governance initiatives depends on a co-ordination mechanism provided by government. Even the more ineffective governments have, none the less, a self-interest in promoting CSR in order to gain the international respectability which can help to attract funding from donors as well as to avoid the need for government intervention, since the private sector can solve problems. But effective CSR can be constrained by the lack of government support, corruption or lack of a civil society. This gives rise to the crucial dilemma that we shall explore in later chapters: government failures can lead to calls for CSR, but effective CSR provision may depend on effective government.

Financial institutions

Financial institutions are important for the oil and gas sector. They provide finance and insurance, including political risk insurance.

They can affect the company as investors/shareholders. In addition, financial institutions can play a quasi-regulatory role – this includes stock exchanges, which establish rules and reporting mechanisms to be followed by listed companies, and the World Bank, which has established various principles that must be followed in projects involving the bank's funding. Furthermore, the global financial oil market has grown significantly over the last decade, with the growth of financial derivates (financial instruments derived from the physical ownership of oil, such as 'futures') and electronic trading; indeed, it has been estimated that the paper value of the financial oil market is ten to twenty times bigger than the actual 80 million barrels of daily physical production of crude oil (James 2006).

Financial institutions have a self-interest in promoting CSR in order to protect their reputations as responsible lenders, as well as helping companies to maintain operations in host countries through creating a more conducive business environment and eliminating risks. Furthermore, there has been a growth of socially responsible investments, which gives institutional investors the leverage to push companies towards certain types of behaviour. In 2006, it was estimated that over €1,000 billion of European investments could be broadly classified as socially responsible investments (an increase from €336 billion in 2003), investments that integrate social, environmental or ethical concerns into investment policies in some form (European Social Investment Forum 2006). Therefore, financial institutions could potentially play a significant role in the introduction and improvement of CSR policies among oil companies.

Non-governmental organisations have often called on banks, the World Bank and export credit agencies to become more socially active and to influence social and environmental practices in the oil and gas sector (Catholic Relief Services 2003; Global Witness 2004). Indeed, international banks and international organisations have come to agree that they need to introduce social and environmental standards relating to the provision of financial services. As a senior World Bank staff member said to the author: 'the onus is on in the next few years how we will lend,' adding that 'the world is moving towards systems of shared governance.'

However, the social and environmental oversight role of financial institutions may be hampered because the social and environmental performance of companies is a secondary goal for them. The primary goal is to earn an economic return, and social and environmental criteria could lead to sub-optimal economic outcomes. The financial institution rarely makes 'the tradeoff between these goals very explicit', while the recipient of funds is primarily accountable for the economic success or failure of the project (Scholtens 2006). Therefore, a single institution has only limited potential for affecting social and environmental behaviour when acting on its own.

The social and environmental role of the World Bank and the IMF is further limited because oil-producing countries are less dependent on the financial assistance of international institutions and Western donors than other developing economies. It is no coincidence that oil-producing countries such as Nigeria, Angola or Venezuela managed to defy the IMF and the World Bank in different ways for a long time. For instance, the oil boom radically improved the bargaining power of Equatorial Guinea, and President Obiang was able to resist calls by the IMF for major macro-economic reforms as a result and to limit the World Bank's involvement in the country (Frynas 2004). As demonstrated in Chapter 6, the World Bank's most far-reaching attempt to maximise the positive social benefits from the oil and gas sector – the revenue management system in Chad – failed because the World Bank lost leverage once oil revenues started flowing to the government of Chad. Even if the World Bank refuses to support a particular project, oil companies and their partners can usually fund projects from alternative sources.

Box 3.1: Equator Principles

The so-called 'Equator Principles' were launched in June 2003 by ten leading international banks from seven countries. The International Finance Corporation (IFC, an arm of the World Bank) played a key role in establishing this initiative, and the Equator Principles were based on World Bank and IFC environmental and social policies and guidelines. Over fifty financial institutions had adopted the principles as of August 2007.

The Equator Principles provide a voluntary set of guidelines for managing social and environmental issues related to project financing with project capital costs over US$10 million. The participating banks commit to using the World Bank/IFC's environmental and social screening process, which categorises projects as A, B, or C (high, medium or low environmental or social risk). For Category A and B projects, the borrower is requested to provide a detailed Social and Environmental Assessment, modelled on existing IFC criteria. In addition, Category A and some Category B projects may require, among other things, an 'action plan', consultation with local stakeholders and a monitoring and reporting procedure.

Further information, see the Equator Principles website at www. equator-principles.com.

Therefore, it is unlikely that a single financial institution can change the social and environmental practices of a specific oil company. Rather, it is hoped that financial institutions can affect the norms and practices within a whole sector. It is hoped, not least among World Bank staff, that the Equator Principles – the key CSR initiative in the financial sector (see Box 3.1) – will have a systemic impact by changing social and environmental norms within the oil and gas industry. As one World Bank staff member stated, the Equator Principles were 'trying to mainstream sustainability concepts amongst clients, especially local firms'. In other words, while the government may remain the most powerful stakeholder, financial institutions are more likely to generate isomorphic pressures with regard to social and environmental policies (compare Chapter 2).

Contractors

Major oil companies have always used some subcontractors, but 'outsourcing' has become even more prevalent over the last two decades. Contractors not only supply crucial equipment such as drilling rigs or pipelines, they also provide oil companies with IT systems and specialised equipment, carry out seismic surveys and drilling operations on their behalf, construct and maintain oil infrastructure and so on. Indeed, some contractors are themselves large multinational companies such as Halliburton, Schlumberger and Aker (see Table 3.2). One could even say that the main function of Shell or Exxon is often to negotiate oil concessions with the host government and to provide a 'co-ordination mechanism' for the exploration and production activities that are carried out on its behalf by a large army of contractors. Indeed, companies such as Shell or Exxon may even outsource technical project management.

In terms of oil exploration and production activities, local communities often have more interactions with contractors than the oil company itself, thus contractors have a self-interest in improved relationships with those communities. Therefore, it is surprising that almost nothing has been written on the social and environmental obligations of contractors in the oil and gas sector. One explanation for this lack of interest may be that the current discussions on CSR focus on global supply chains and assume that the large multinational firms are responsible for the behaviour of the suppliers/ contractors with whom they do business (Acona 2004; Barrientos and Smith 2007; MacDonald 2007; Newell and Wheeler 2006). This can help to explain why contractors are rarely in the media spotlight and tend to face fewer stakeholder pressures for implementing social and environmental improvements.

There is much support for the argument that multinational firms wield a lot of power over their suppliers of products and services, and their suppliers may adopt CSR just to continue a business relationship

TABLE 3.2: *The world's largest oil and gas service multinational companies, by foreign assets, 2005 (in US$ million)*

Rank	Company	Home country	Foreign assets	Total assets	Foreign sales	Total sales	Number of employees
1	Schlumberger	United States	11,272.0	17,746.0	10,436.0	14,309.0	60,000
2	Halliburton	United States	6,562.4	15,048.0	15,339.0	21,007.0	106,000
3	Aker	Norway	5,159.0	8,131.2	6,297.5	9,172.6	37,000
4	Weatherford International	United States	4,587.9	8,580.3	2,724.0	4,333.2	25,100
5	Transocean	United States	4,437.0	10,457.2	2,244.0	2,891.7	9,600
6	Noble Corporation	United States	3,208.1	4,346.4	1,067.3	1,382.1	5,600
7	Pride International	United States	2,950.9	4,086.5	1,766.9	2,033.3	12,200
8	Globalsantafe Corporation	United States	2,754.6	6,193.9	1,583.7	2,263.5	5,700
9	Nabors Industries	United States	1,755.3	7,230.4	1,169.5	3,459.9	22,599
10	Ensco International	United States	1,603.6	3,614.1	620.1	1,046.9	3,700

Source: United Nations Conference on Trade and Development 2007, 118.

with the multinational company. Indeed, CSR initiatives such as codes of conduct are often imposed on a supplier by its customer – the multinational firm. None the less, it has also been shown that those externally imposed CSR initiatives such as ethical codes of conduct are often not effectively implemented by the supplier of even the more socially responsible multinational firms, especially if the volume of business is relatively small between the supplier and the client multinational firm (Barrientos and Smith 2007). Furthermore, suppliers are often less concerned with their external reputation, as they are smaller in size and depend less on brands and marketing to end-consumers. As a result of these limitations, in the most extreme case of China, it has been reported that as many as '95% of export oriented [supplier] factories in China [are] said to falsify records used in monitoring labour standards' (Blowfield 2007). Suppliers/contractors thus continue to exert an important influence on the social and environmental practices that are actually applied in their operations, independently of their clients' social and environmental policies.

In addition to hiring contractors to provide commercial products and services, oil companies may also hire contractors to implement CSR-related initiatives, including social and environmental consultants (e.g., for devising CSR schemes), environmental remedy firms (e.g., for cleaning up oil spills), development specialists (e.g., for executing local community development projects) and so on. The author has encountered a number of instances where an oil company regarded as 'less responsible' was able to execute a better CSR initiative than the 'more responsible' company thanks to hiring better contractors and vice versa. Therefore, the choice of contractors can significantly influence the quality of a company's CSR initiatives.

Non-governmental organisations

A non-governmental organisation (NGO) may be simply defined as a not-for-profit pressure group (Thompson-Feraru 1974), a definition that covers the many human rights, environmental or local community groups that target oil companies. The key characteristic of NGOs is that they are independent of government and herein lies their strength. While governments must perform many functions, an NGO can often concentrate on a single issue to the exclusion of all others, therefore, 'NGOs can apply their resources' in a way 'that is more focused than the attention and resources that state representatives may be able to devote to the same issues'. Furthermore, in taking up principle-based issues, NGOs can claim legitimacy and affect public opinion at both the domestic and international levels (Clark 1995).

NGOs have campaigned on oil-related issues (especially marine pollution) since at least the 1920s, when groups such as the National Coast Anti-Pollution League in the USA and the Royal Society for the Protection of Birds (RSPB) in the UK lobbied for oil pollution legislation. NGOs are, of course, very diverse and can range from a large multinational organisation like Greenpeace, with affiliate groups in dozens of countries, to a small group of concerned local citizens in a village. From the mid-1990s, a significant number of internationally operating NGOs campaigned on issues related to the oil and gas industry, which included a diverse range of groups such as Greenpeace, Friends of the Earth, Catholic Relief Services, Global Witness, BUND and many others. A number of NGOs have dedicated all or most of their work to domestic oil and gas sector activities, including a number of groups based in developing economies such as MOSOP in Nigeria or Kazakhstan Revenue Watch, but their influence has usually been local and limited compared with the larger international NGOs such as Greenpeace.

While the impact of NGOs is difficult to quantify and the NGOs have a self-interest in exaggerating their own impact, there is evidence that NGOs can impact policy, especially if they enter issue-specific alliances (Warleigh 2000). Notable examples of successful NGO campaigns in the oil and gas sector included Greenpeace's campaign against Shell's Brent Spar platform in 1995 (Rice and Owen 1999; Zyglidopoulos 2002), and the contribution of NGOs to the development of policy initiatives such as the Extractive Industry's Transparency Initiative (EITI) and the Voluntary Principles on Security and Human Rights (Freeman 2001; Publish What You Pay and Revenue Watch Institute 2006).

Beyond NGO campaigns against oil firms, the last decade has also seen a rise in partnerships between companies and NGOs (Bendell 2000; Svendsen and Laberge 2005). These partnerships have taken many forms. Sometimes firms may engage with an NGO for a specific project, for instance for marketing an environmentally friendly product. At other times, many firms form a formal coalition with various NGOs on general issues of joint interest. In the oil and gas sector, companies have often forged partnerships comprising NGOs and local communities, aimed at local community development in developing economies (see Chapter 5). These partnerships can sometimes blur the difference between an NGO and a paid contractor in cases where the NGO engages in a specific project that is directly funded by the company. Working in partnerships towards the establishment of CSR standards and principles, oil companies and NGOs have also collaborated in initiatives such as the United Nations Global Compact and the above-mentioned EITI. Companies have various reasons for entering such partnerships, including the desire to use NGOs to gain credibility and to solve operational problems.

While some NGOs have been highly critical of CSR initiatives or have even rejected the notion of voluntary CSR and self-regulation (Christian Aid 2004; International Council on Human Rights Policy 2002), NGOs have an interest in engaging with CSR, not least since CSR can represent shared goals with the business community, engagement with CSR can help NGOs to secure funding and NGOs are able to influence the emerging CSR standards, codes and 'social norms'. The key limitation of NGOs is their lack of accountability compared with government or democratic trade unions, their lack of grassroots support and their ineffectiveness at providing services (Blowfield and Murray 2008, 258). In sum, NGOs seek to and are able to influence various CSR initiatives, but their legitimacy and capacity are often limited.

Conclusion

An analysis of the industry context demonstrates that the attribution of social responsibility to a specific actor can often be complex, especially if the government and contractors have significant influence over day-to-day business operations. Even if a company like Shell controls all activities along the supply chain and can be held directly responsible for an oil spill or adverse social effects, questions may be asked about the partial responsibility of financial institutions or the government for the company's operations. An analysis of the context of CSR implies that a narrow focus on 'corporate' responsibility can be misguided, and an investigation of corporate responsibilities must be accompanied by an investigation of the responsibilities of government and the responsibilities of financial institutions.

The analysis of the context in this industry also implies that the nature of oil and gas operations involves many potential negative social and environmental effects, ranging from the negative effects of seismic studies to oil spills during transportation and processing of oil. On the one hand, oil operations can cause environmental damage at different stages of the supply chain. Accordingly, Chapter 4 will discuss environmental issues in greater depth. On the other hand, oil operations involve many interactions between multinational companies and local people in often remote rural areas. Accordingly, Chapter 5 will address local community issues.

At this point, we must stress that the industry context does not by itself shape the conduct of companies. As the previous chapter demonstrated, the CSR strategies of firms are also shaped by the national context, specific stakeholder groups and the attitudes of the corporate decision-makers. Human action can play a role, and a personal decision by a company's director or an asset manager can also influence the direction of a company.

Therefore, the industry context cannot explain why the oil and gas industry has applied different operating standards around the world, why Shell has been more active in CSR than other oil companies or why a specific corporate decision was taken on a given occasion. But the industry context can help to explain why the oil and gas industry has been more heavily criticised by NGOs for its operations than other industries and, as a result of such criticism, why multinational oil companies have become active CSR advocates. It can help to explain why local community development has been a key issue for oil companies, whereas it rarely features as a prominent issue for many other types of companies. It can also help to explain some of the difficulties that oil companies have had in executing CSR initiatives in the face of constraints posed by government policy or in the absence of government intervention. As we stated at the outset of this chapter, the success of CSR initiatives is highly dependent on the context.

FOUR

The environmental challenge

By looking at CSR's prospects and limitations in the oil and gas sector this chapter investigates the extent to which CSR can address environmental challenges. As indicated in Chapter 3, the environmental challenge of the oil and gas industry lies in the fact that the nature of oil operations involves many potential negative environmental effects. Public awareness of the environmental impact of oil operations was heightened by major environmental disasters in the past, including oil tanker accidents such as the *Exxon Valdez* spill off Alaska in 1989 and 'well blow-outs', for example, when Mexico's Ixtoc 1 oil well blew out and released an estimated 3 million barrels of oil into the Gulf of Mexico in 1979.

As mentioned in Chapter 3, oil and gas operations pose a threat to the environment at each stage of the process – construction, exploration, production, transportation and refining. During the construction of oil infrastructure and oil company facilities, lorries and construction teams may cause dust and waste may be created. During the exploration for oil and gas, environmental threats include, among others, clearance of land (which can lead to a long-lasting or permanent loss of vegetation) and drilling activities (which can lead to the release of drilling fluids). Oil production activities can have an adverse impact on the environment through damage from leaking pipelines or atmospheric emissions from the flaring of gas, a by-product of oil production. During transportation, tankers release oil into the sea in the course of pumping out bilge-water or unloading the cargo. The pollution from refineries can include the release of waste water containing oil residuals, solid waste disposal and atmospheric emissions. In addition to the eco-logical hazards in the course of oil operations, end-user consump-tion of oil products – together with other fossil fuels – is an important contributor to global warming (Clark 1982; Estrada et al. 1997; White 2002). Table 4.1 provides an overview of the potential environmental impact of oil companies and the potential mitigating activities.

The potential environmental impact of oil and gas operations is greatest during the production phase (see Table 4.2). However, the impact of oil and gas operations greatly varies between different locations. In some areas, such as farmland and uncultivated bush areas, the environmental effects may be relatively insignificant. In other areas, however, oil and gas operations may leave long-term damage. For instance, in mangrove swamps, it may take two to three years for mangrove bushes to recover after their roots have been cut into, and it may take thirty years or more for mangrove trees to fully recover from a seismic survey (Frynas 2000, 158). Environmental risks of oil and gas operations are heightened because in developing economies natural resources, including oil and gas deposits, are often located near areas of high biological diversity and high ecological vulnerability, such as rain forests, mangrove swamps and protected national parks (Austin and Sauer 2002).

In this chapter, we shall not discuss environmental risks in detail, but rather evaluate the extent to which CSR can address the environ-mental impact of company operations.

TABLE 4.1: *Overview of environmental impact of oil companies and mitigating activities*

Process stage	Design and construction	Exploration and production	Transportation	Refining and processing	End use
Impact	Dust Light Noise Waste	Air emissions Greenhouse gases Light Noise Waste Water	Air emissions Greenhouse gases Noise Waste Water	Air emissions Greenhouse gases Light Noise Waste Water	Air emissions Greenhouse gases
Mitigating activity	Dust, light and noise impact minimisation Footprint minimisation Traffic management Waste management	Drilling discharge management Energy efficiency Gas flare minimisation Pipeline integrity management Waste/Water management Water/gas reinjection	Double-hull tankers Pipeline integrity management	Catalyst regeneration Clean fuels Cogeneration Energy efficiency Flare minimisation Fuel gas sulphur reduction Furnace NOx mitigation Waste/Water management	Inventory and supply chain optimisation Underground storage tank integrity Vapour recovery

Source: adapted from the Chevron website at www.chevron.com (accessed 13 February 2008).

TABLE 4.2: *Potential environmental impact of oil production activities*

Production activity	Potential environmental impact
All activities	Loss of vegetation/arable land Hydrological changes Disturbance of communities/flora/fauna
Well operations	Soil, water pollution Disturbance of communities/flora/fauna
Pipelines	Soil, water pollution Disturbance of communities/flora/fauna
Separation of oil/gas/water	Ambient air quality Acid rain Soot/heavy metal deposition Greenhouse effect Pollution/fire affecting flora Soil/surface water pollution Disturbance of communities/flora/fauna
Oil terminals	Soil/surface water pollution Disturbance of communities/flora/fauna Poor ambient air quality Ozone depletion (fire-fighting agents) Soil, water, air pollution Waste problems Soil pollution

Source: adapted from van Dessel 1995.

Tackling the environmental challenge

While the use of terms such as 'CSR' and 'Sustainability' is relatively new, oil companies were prepared to voluntarily introduce some pollution-related initiatives from at least the 1960s. Already in 1969, oil companies established an industry-wide voluntary agreement called the Tanker Owners' Voluntary Agreement concerning Liability for Oil Pollution (referred to as TOVALOP), and in 1974 the Offshore Pollution Liability Agreement (referred to as OPOL) was set up to meet claims for marine pollution damage and environmental clean-up costs. Under the terms of these agreements, oil companies voluntarily accepted strict liability for pollution damage and the cost of remedial measures. However, much of the public attention to oil companies was focused on marine pollution at the time. With the general rise in environmental awareness around the world since the 1970s, the quantity and scope of voluntary environmental initiatives have greatly increased, and the environmental agenda has widened to include broader issues such as climate change and biodiversity.

As one of the key signs of environmental engagement, oil companies now provide extensive environmental reports. Indeed, several comparative international studies have demonstrated that environmental reporting among oil and gas companies is more extensive compared with other sectors, including utilities and various branches of manufacturing, although this has partly been a result of the industry's greater environmental impact. In addition, a high percentage of oil companies use third-party verification of their environmental reports, compared with companies in most other sectors (Kolk *et al.* 2001). According to the 2005 survey of CSR reporting by the consultancy firm KPMG, 16 out of 20 oil and gas companies listed among the 250 largest corporations in the world reported on corporate responsibility issues, which represented a significant increase from 58 per cent to 80 per cent between 2002 and 2005 (KPMG 2005).

Steps have also been taken to create common environmental reporting standards tailored to the needs of the oil and gas sector. In 2005, the International Petroleum Industry Environmental Conservation Association (an organisation representing oil companies and associations from around the world) and the American Petroleum Institute (a trade association representing oil companies in the United States) issued the 'Oil and Gas Industry Guidance on Voluntary Sustainability Reporting'. The guidance includes six core environmental performance indicators and nine supplementary indicators, in addition to health and safety, social and economic indicators. For each environmental indicator, a specific guideline and a unit of measurement (e.g., gigajoules for energy use) is provided.

The 2005 Oil and Gas Guidance is not as comprehensive as the reporting guidelines of the Global Reporting Initiative (GRI), which comprise seventeen core environmental indicators and thirteen supplementary indicators (see Table 4.3 for a comparison). However, while the GRI provides generic indicators suitable for any type of industry, the Oil and Gas Guidance is much more specific to the oil and gas sector and comprises indicators including 'hydrocarbon spills' and 'flared and vented gas'. The 2005 Guidance is thus more useful for addressing the specific industry context. Before the Guidance was created, a World Bank staff member interviewed by the author in Washington, DC in 2004 commented: 'The oil and gas companies would benefit from a more robust system [of social and environmental industry standards] that's relevant to them.'

The author of this book has analysed recent social and environmental reports published by twenty oil and gas companies to ascertain the use of the 'core' environmental indicators from the 2005 Oil and Gas Guidance in practice. The analysis covered the reports of ten Western multinational companies (Shell, BP, Chevron, Exxon, Statoil, Norsk Hydro, Total, ENI, Repsol and OMV) and ten multinational companies from emerging markets (China National Offshore Oil Corporation/CNOOC, China Petroleum & Chemical Corporation/Sinopec, Lukoil, Gazprom, MOL, Petrobras, Petronas, PKN Orlen, PTT and Sasol).[1] The results are summarised in Table 4.4. 'Reported' information means that the exact figures or data has been provided by the company. 'Limited' information means that either no exact figures or no precise information has been provided (e.g., related information, a graph without a specific figure

---

[1] The 2006 data were used for 18 companies. As a result of the unavailability of the 2006 report, 2005 data were used for CNOOC and 2007 data for Petronas.

TABLE 4.3: *Comparison of environmental performance indicators*

Category	Indicator	2005 Oil Guidance	GRI Guidelines
Water	Freshwater use	Additional	–
	Total water withdrawal	–	Core
	Water sources affected by withdrawal	–	Additional
	Recycled and reused water	–	Additional
Spills/ discharges	Hydrocarbon spills to the environment	Core	–
	Discharges to water	Core	Core
	Water/habitats affected by discharges to water	–	Additional
	Other spills and accidental releases	Additional	Core
	Other effluent discharges	Additional	–
Waste	Total waste	–	Core
	Hazardous waste	Additional	Additional
	Non-hazardous waste	Additional	–
Materials	Materials used	–	Core
	Recycled, reused or reclaimed materials	Additional	Core
Emissions	Greenhouse gas emissions	Core	Core
	Indirect greenhouse gas emissions	–	Core
	Initiatives to reduce greenhouse gas emissions	–	Additional
	Emissions of Ozone-Depleting Substances	–	Core
	Other operational air emissions	Additional	Core
	Flared and vented gas	Core	–
Resource use	Primary energy use	Core	Core
	Indirect energy consumption	–	Core
	Reductions in indirect energy consumption	–	Additional
	Energy savings from conservation and efficiency improvements	–	Additional
	New and renewable energy resources	Additional	Additional
Biodiversity	Location and size of land with high biodiversity value	–	Core
	Description of impact of activities	–	Core
	Habitats protected or restored	–	Additional

TABLE 4.3: (cont.)

Category	Indicator	2005 Oil Guidance	GRI Guidelines
	Initiatives for managing biodiversity	Additional	Additional
	Protected species with habitats in areas affected by operations	–	Additional
Products and services	Mitigation of environmental impacts of products and services	–	Core
	Reclaimed products and packaging materials	–	Core
Other indicators	Fines for non-compliance with environmental laws and regulations	–	Core
	Environmental impact of transport	–	Additional
	Environmental protection expenditures	–	Additional
	Environmental management systems	Core	–

Sources: www.oilandgasreporting.com and www.globalreporting.org (accessed 25 February 2008).

for effluents or no precise information on the application of the ISO 14001 standard).

The analysis of environmental reporting suggests that it is still not possible to systematically compare the environmental performance of different multinational oil companies, even using the main recommended indicators. The 2005 Oil and Gas Guidance is not followed across the sector and there is sometimes a lack of clarity with regard to which standards are actually used by companies. A number of companies such as South Africa's Sasol make explicit use of the reporting guidelines of the Global Reporting Initiative, not the 2005 Oil and Gas Guidance.

The most regularly reported environmental indicator is the total greenhouse gas emissions, and it is possible to compare company performance on greenhouse gas emissions across the sector.

TABLE 4.4: *Core environmental indicators reported by selected oil companies in 2006*

Company	Country	Hydrocarbon spills	Discharges to water	Core environmental indicators Greenhouse emissions	Flared gas	Energy use	Environmental management systems
BP	UK	REPORTED	REPORTED	REPORTED	REPORTED	REPORTED	REPORTED
Shell	UK	LIMITED	LIMITED	REPORTED	REPORTED	LIMITED	LIMITED
Chevron	USA	REPORTED	–	REPORTED	LIMITED	REPORTED	REPORTED
Exxon	USA	REPORTED	REPORTED	REPORTED	REPORTED	REPORTED	LIMITED
Statoil	Norway	LIMITED	LIMITED	LIMITED	REPORTED	REPORTED	–
Norsk Hydro	Norway	LIMITED	LIMITED	REPORTED	LIMITED	REPORTED	–
Total	France	REPORTED	REPORTED	REPORTED	REPORTED	REPORTED	LIMITED
ENI	Italy	REPORTED	LIMITED	LIMITED	LIMITED	REPORTED	REPORTED
Repsol	Spain	REPORTED	REPORTED	REPORTED	–	REPORTED	REPORTED
OMV	Austria	LIMITED	REPORTED	REPORTED	–	REPORTED	LIMITED

| Company | Country | Core environmental indicators | | | | | |
		Hydrocarbon spills	Discharges to water	Greenhouse emissions	Flared gas	Energy use	Environmental management systems
CNOOC*	China	–	LIMITED	–	–	–	LIMITED
Sinopec	China	–	LIMITED	LIMITED	LIMITED	LIMITED	LIMITED
Lukoil	Russia	–	LIMITED	–	–	–	LIMITED
Gazprom	Russia	–	LIMITED	REPORTED	–	–	LIMITED
MOL	Hungary	LIMITED	REPORTED	REPORTED	–	REPORTED	LIMITED
Petrobras	Brazil	LIMITED	–	REPORTED	LIMITED	REPORTED	REPORTED
Petronas**	Malaysia	–	–	–	–	–	REPORTED
PKN Orlen	Poland	–	–	–	–	–	LIMITED
PTT	Thailand	LIMITED	LIMITED	REPORTED	–	–	LIMITED
Sasol	South Africa	–	LIMITED	REPORTED	–	REPORTED	LIMITED

Notes: * 2005 data were used for CNOOC because of the unavailability of the 2006 report.
** 2007 data were used for Petronas because of the unavailability of the 2006 report.

However, the widespread reporting on greenhouse gas emissions is rather exceptional and is related to rising environmental concerns over global climate change. With regard to other environmental indicators such as 'flared gas', it is difficult to make comparisons across the sector.

BP, Exxon and Total appear to follow the 2005 Oil and Gas Guidance most closely, although other companies also provide a substantial quantity of data; for instance, Shell fails to provide exact figures on discharges to water, but the company provides annual figures on hazardous waste and freshwater use. One can also see continued improvements in environmental reporting; for instance, Chevron began to collect data on water and waste performance in 2006, which the company had previously not collected at the corporate level.

With regard to emerging market companies, there are huge differences in environmental reporting and environmental practices between different companies. Brazil's Petrobras, South Africa's Sasol and Hungary's MOL have particularly sophisticated reporting mechanisms and sophisticated environmental management systems. In contrast, the Chinese oil company CNOOC and the Malaysian oil company Petronas not only have underdeveloped reporting mechanisms but also do not seem to address a number of important environmental issues in their operations.

In general, emerging market companies have less developed environmental reporting, and even the best performers lack clear, uniform reporting standards. None the less, one needs to remember that the annual reporting of environmental data and the 2005 Oil and Gas Guidance are relatively new and companies continue to make improvements to their standards of reporting. Most importantly, the recent developments in environmental reporting allow us to see some areas where oil companies have made environmental improvements and a number of areas where they have so far failed to make improvements.

Obviously, environmental reporting is merely a means to an end, with the end being improved environmental practices. The reports allow us to trace performance over time and they provide evidence that oil companies have made some improvements in their environmental performance over the years. For instance, Shell has reported a decrease in the volume of oil spills from 19.3 to 5.7 thousand tonnes between 1997 and 2006 (a 70 per cent decline), while Chevron has reported a decrease in the volume of oil spills from 54,696 to 6,099 barrels between 2002 and 2006 (a decline of almost 90 per cent).

A crucial area of recent environmental concern has been greenhouse gas emissions and their contribution to global warming. An important contributor to carbon dioxide emissions has been the flaring of associated gas during oil-production activities in developing economies, and some oil companies have made major progress on reducing gas flaring. For instance, Mexico's Pemex is said to have reduced flared gas from 6,821 to 3,586 million cubic metres between 1998 and 2001 (World Bank 2004), while Shell planned to reduce gas flaring from its operations in Nigeria to 15 per cent of the total associated gas produced by about 2010, from a level of 65 per cent in 1997 (Shell Nigeria 2007; Frynas 2000, 164). Shell reportedly reduced its total greenhouse gas emissions from 109 to 98 million tonnes of carbon dioxide equivalent in the period 1997–2006, while BP's total greenhouse gas emissions have decreased from 82.4 to 64.6 million tonnes of carbon dioxide equivalent between 2002 and 2006.

Another important indicator of environmental performance is the number of oil spills above one barrel of oil (159 litres). The incidence of oil spills is not strictly comparable year-by-year because it can be affected by levels of production and by natural disasters (e.g., hurricanes in 2005), and the volume of oil spills in a given year can be affected by a particularly big oil spill. None the less, the 2002–6 comparison of oil spill data suggests that companies are progressively reducing the number of oil spills. Of the four big oil majors, BP, Exxon and Chevron have reduced the number of oil spills; Shell did not

TABLE 4.5: *Number of oil spills by selected companies, 2002–6*

	2002	2003	2004	2005	2006
BP	761	635	578	541	417
Chevron	1,502	1,145	986	846	803
Exxon	n/a	466	475	370	295
Norsk Hydro	87	70	54	70	75
Petrobras	197	276	530	269	293

provide figures for the number of oil spills, but the volume of oil spills has declined from 7.4 to 5.7 thousand tonnes. The only emerging market company for which 2002–6 data were available (Petrobras) reported an increase in oil spills (see Table 4.5).

The most impressive evidence on environmental improvements in the oil and gas sector is provided by a historical comparison of oil spills from oil tankers. Since the 1970s, the number of large oil spills (above 700 tonnes) caused by oil tankers and other vessels has dramatically decreased, from 25.2 spills per year in the period 1970–9 to 3.6 spills per year in the period 2000–7. During the 1970s a figure of about thirty major oil spills per year was not unusual. During the period 2000–7, the highest annual number of major oil spills was five (2004). The volume of oil spills has also dramatically decreased over the last three decades, except for the year 2002, when the Greek-owned oil tanker *Prestige* sank off the coast of Spain (see Figures 4.1 and 4.2).

The data presented above suggest that oil companies have made significant environmental improvements, although environmental improvements have not been unequivocal. For instance, company reports show that Exxon's total greenhouse gas emissions increased by 6 per cent between 2002 and 2006, while the hazardous waste generated by Shell more than doubled between 1998 and 2006. BP was fined US$50 million by the US Government for an explosion at a Texas oil refinery in 2005, and the company pleaded guilty to US

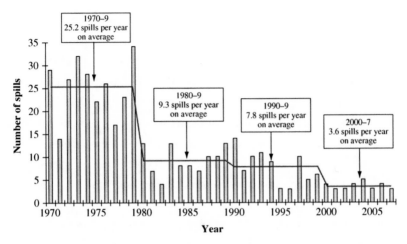

Figure 4.1: Number of marine oil spills over 700 tonnes, 1970–2007
Source: The International Tanker Owners Pollution Federation website at www.itopf.com (accessed 27 February 2008).

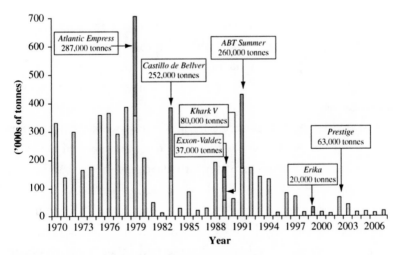

Figure 4.2: Quantity of marine oil spills (tonnes), 1970-2007
Source: The International Tanker Owners Pollution Federation website at www.itopf.com (accessed 27 February 2008).

criminal environmental charges, while BP also faced criticism over other environmental practices in the United States, including the safety of its pipelines in Alaska (Davis *et al.* 2007). Above all, there is evidence that even the 'best-in-class' Western multinationals have used substandard environmental practices in their operations in developing economies, including showcase projects such as the BP-led Baku–Tbilisi pipeline project – an oil pipeline from Azerbaijan to Turkey (Thornton 2004). Furthermore, the previous discussion suggests that environmental improvements among emerging market companies have been rather limited.

None the less, the improvements that have been achieved deserve credit and it may be useful to ask why improvements were possible.

The basis of environmental success

The success of CSR in addressing various environmental issues can be explained by the convergence of environmental and business interests. Both companies and the environment can benefit from energy efficiency and a reduction in gas flaring, as the sale of previously flared natural gas or energy savings can lead to better financial performance.

Indeed, the general evidence for a business case or win-win outcomes of CSR is strongest with regard to environmental issues, as opposed to 'social' issues such as health and safety, labour standards or local development. Findings by the organisation SustainAbility show that the most demonstrable business benefits from CSR are in the area of eco-efficiency, which includes reduction in the use of materials and emissions, recycling and reuse and other 'new' practices. These relatively 'new' practices have been shown to increase shareholder value, operational efficiency, access to capital and improved reputation (SustainAbility 2001, 2002). The investment group Innovest has asserted that 85 per cent of studies show a positive correlation between environmental governance and financial performance (Innovest and Environment Agency 2004) (reported in Blowfield and Murray 2008, 132–3 and 138–42).

Interviewed oil company managers and engineers have narrated various examples of instances when they were proud of their company's environmental improvements, for instance reducing carbon dioxide emissions, implementing a zero-spill policy for the company or replacing steel tubes with chrome tubes. In many instances, company staff discovered that there was a convergence of environmental and business interests. For instance, one oil company engineer pointed out that a steel tube may only last for several years in a tropical environment, whereas a chrome tube may last for twenty years; therefore, the use of better quality materials or better quality equipment helps an oil company both to reduce the likelihood of environmental damage and to reduce the necessity for business interventions in future.

Furthermore, previous studies have concluded that environmental improvements can help companies to innovate. One study compared seven Canadian oil companies and found that the two companies most proactive on environmental improvements (Buffalo Oil and Sioux Oil) greatly benefited from related innovations such as technology patents in the areas of process improvement, sulphur dioxide recovery, waste reduction and disposal, soil restoration and less polluting fuels. In turn, innovations helped the development of new revenue streams for those companies, such as sales of less polluting fuels (Sharma and Vredenburg 1998). Statistical analyses further support the view that the diffusion of environmentally friendly technology enhances innovation (Bhatnagar and Cohen 1997; Lanjouw and Mody 1996). This type of empirical evidence complements the new ideas of management thinkers such as Michael Porter, who assert that environmental competences can lead to competitive advantages in business (Porter 1991; Porter and Kramer 2006; Porter and van der Linde 1995).

Interview data also suggest that companies have been successful at environmental improvements because the technical and managerial capabilities of oil companies are particularly suited to addressing environmental issues. As the author of this book has previously argued, when environmental improvements can be reduced to distinct technical tasks, oil companies can perform CSR tasks to a high standard (Frynas 2005). Environmental improvements such as new oil pipelines, improved forms of combustion or new production processes require similar engineering and managerial skills to those needed by oil companies in their commercial day-to-day operations, for instance increasing production levels or reducing production costs. Technical problems need to be solved, new production processes and patents need to be developed, project teams need to be formed and so on.

BP's efforts to reduce greenhouse gas emissions, led by the company's chief executive John Browne (BP's CEO between 1995 and 2007), demonstrate the strength of companies in tackling environmental issues. In 1997, BP set itself the target of reducing greenhouse gas emissions from its own facilities by 10 per cent from 1990 levels by 2010. The company was able to attain this goal nine years early at the end of 2001. The company then set itself a new target of ensuring that net emissions do not increase between 2001 to 2012 (Henderson Global Investors 2005). Since 2001, BP has made further progress. According to the company's 2006 Sustainability Report, BP's greenhouse gas emissions declined by a further 22 per cent between 2002 and 2006, while the company's oil production increased in the same period by over 30 per cent and its natural gas production almost doubled.

BP's quick success in reducing emissions has often been attributed to the introduction in January 2000 of an emissions trading system within the company, which gave BP's subsidiaries the freedom to decide how to address emissions reductions within their organisational unit in the most cost-effective manner (see Box 4.1). The technical and managerial skills of BP's staff underpinned BP's climate-change effort. In the words of a former BP manager, the company's staff reportedly 'worked hard' and 'enjoyed the technical

Box 4.1: BP's emissions trading system

In 1997, BP's CEO John Browne announced that BP would drastically reduce its greenhouse gas emissions, and the company decided to use internal emissions trading to deliver emissions reductions. In preparation for the launch of the trading system, a pilot project was started in 1998, while carbon dioxide and methane emissions were systematically and reliably measured across BP's operations as a crucial precondition of successful emissions trading.

Each business unit was assigned a target for the emission of greenhouse gases and a number of 'permits', each of which gave the business unit the right to emit one tonne of carbon dioxide. BP's business units were able to trade permits among themselves. A business unit that was able to reduce greenhouse gas emissions was free to sell permits. A business unit that was unable to find economical methods of reducing emissions could buy permits. Therefore, the trading system introduced incentives for pursuing the most cost-effective methods for emissions reductions within the company as a whole.

A significant part of the emissions reduction was achieved through reductions in gas flaring and venting. BP estimated that the company was able to save US$650 million through decreased gas venting and flaring, either by selling the gas or by increased energy efficiency.

The emissions trading system was operational from January 2000 until the end of 2001, by which time BP had achieved a 10 per cent reduction in greenhouse gas emissions.

Sources: Akhurst *et al.* 2003; Malone 2004; Victor and House 2006.

challenge' of making improvements to plant and equipment. In general terms, this example helps to explain why companies are particularly skilled at dealing with environmental challenges that are measurable, in contrast to their lack of skills in dealing with social challenges that are difficult to measure (see Chapter 5).

BP's efforts to reduce gas emissions are even more impressive, given that the company was able to reduce emissions at a time when its commercial operations were actually expanding. In the period 2002–6, when gas emissions declined by 22 per cent, the company's crude oil

TABLE 4.6: *Changes in greenhouse gas emissions and production levels by selected companies, 2002–6 (percentages)*

	Change in greenhouse gas emissions	Change in crude oil production	Change in natural gas production
BP	−22	+32	+94
Norsk Hydro	−14	+15	+38
Shell	−8	−14	−10
Chevron[*]	−2	−9	+13
Exxon[**]	+6	0	−8
Gazprom	+20	+328	+7
Repsol	+21	−10	+45
OMV[***]	+24	+45	n/a
Petrobras	+66	+25	+37

Notes: * 2002–5 change, 2006 data not comparable as a result of the purchase of Unocal by Chevron in August 2005.
** 2003–6 change, 2002 data not available.
*** 2002–5 change, 2006 data is not comparable as a result of the purchase of Romania's Petrom by OMV; 45 per cent is a combined figure for oil and natural gas production.

and natural gas production increased by 32 per cent and 94 per cent, respectively. The Norwegian company Norsk Hydro was the only other company able to achieve significant reductions in emissions despite an increase in oil and gas production. The other companies' performance was far less impressive than that of BP and Norsk Hydro. Shell's and Chevron's gas emissions also declined from 2002 to 2006, but this could be attributed to declining oil production. The gas emissions of other companies such as Exxon and Repsol have actually increased significantly (see Table 4.6).

The contrast between the performance of BP and the other companies points to the importance of the corporate will and the need for changes to internal management systems for achieving environmental improvements. Even if examples such as BP and Norsk Hydro are an exception rather than the rule, they demonstrate the great ability of multinational companies to restructure internal operations and redeploy resources in order to achieve significant improvements in environmental performance.

None the less, our discussion also demonstrates the constraints to the current CSR agenda: lack of convergence of reporting standards, the huge variations in environmental practices between different companies and the lack of progress on key environmental indicators by many companies. Therefore, there are limitations on voluntary measures to tackle the environmental challenges, which will be discussed in the rest of the chapter.

The limitations of corporate environmentalism

This section does not attempt to dismiss the environmental improvements made by companies, but rather aims to understand the limitations of the current CSR agenda. We shall discuss the three main limitations of CSR revealed by existing research: limitations of environmental reporting, regulatory constraints and end-user consumption of oil.

Limitations of environmental reporting

There is a recognition that CSR reports are better at covering environmental issues than social ones and environmental reporting has been practised by companies for longer than social reporting (Blowfield 2007; KPMG 2005). Yet criticism of corporate reporting comes both from academics and mainstream organisations such as the Association of Chartered Certified Accountants (ACCA).

Despite the standardisation of environmental reporting mentioned earlier, there is evidence that corporate reporting has provided stakeholders with relatively little useful data. A recent study that analysed the links between corporate reporting and the environmental perform-ance of nine oil companies concluded that corporate reports have three key shortcomings: (1) specific performance metrics are often absent; (2) the available data do not allow comparability between companies; and (3) CSR commitments cannot be readily related to the environmental outcomes that are achieved or not achieved (Gouldson and Sullivan 2007, 10).

Even among the sustainability 'leaders' in the oil and gas sector such as BP and Shell, it was not possible to systematically compare the environmental performance between companies. Companies some-times measure different things and sometimes use different units of measurement for the same environmental indicators.

Furthermore, while companies provided macro-level data (e.g., on global greenhouse gas emissions), they often failed to provide data on specific locations (e.g., a specific refinery). In the words of Andy Gouldson and Rory Sullivan, 'even the leading companies in the sector examined rarely disclosed site-level data and, where they did so, these data were not provided on a consistent basis or in a common format' (Gouldson and Sullivan 2007, 5).

Most worryingly, while environmental indicators such as emissions levels are reported by companies, there is almost no emphasis on the actual impact on the natural and human environment. The study by Gouldson and Sullivan concluded:

> Within the corporate and site level reports, little or no reference was made to key outcomes such as levels of local air quality or the health of local populations ... The focus on emissions rather than, for example, local air quality, also meant that it was impos-sible to evaluate social or environmental outcomes at the local level, thereby restricting the ability of stakeholders to make informed decisions or to focus their engagement with the com-panies on individual sites or on particular aspects of their performance. (Gouldson and Sullivan 2007, 5)

Michael Blowfield from the University of Oxford Smith School of Enterprise and the Environment recently assessed the existing information on the social and environmental impact of companies. Blowfield's conclusions echoed those of Gouldson and Sullivan:

> We know much more about the business case, and company attitudes, awareness and practices, than we do about how CSR affects the major areas of social and environmental change where its proponents claim it has an impact. (Blowfield 2007, 693)

Therefore, we know how companies such as Shell or BP are improving their overall environmental performance and whether they achieve their own targets (e.g., for reductions in greenhouse gas emissions), but there are no systematic attempts to measure the actual impact of oil operations on air quality, water quality or the health of local communities. The local stakeholders – for instance, the local residents who live near an oil refinery or a drilling rig – are not provided with the specific information that is most vital to them.

While companies such as Shell and BP provide at least some tangible data on their environmental performance, the quality of reporting by some companies is highly superficial. In particular, many oil companies from developing economies provide little concrete data on social and environmental issues, as the examples of China's CNOOC and Malaysia's Petronas demonstrate. The 2005 CSR report by CNOOC (running to forty pages) provides only figures on produced water, while the 2007 sustainability report by Petronas fails to provide any environmental indicators (see Table 4.4).

The introduction of CSR or sustainability reports by many firms from developing economies (such as CNOOC or Petronas) suggests that there has been some imitation of Western practices in line with the 'isomorphic pressures' discussed in Chapter 2. Indeed, KPMG predicted that social and environmental reporting by developing nation firms will continue to expand, as more firms will seek a listing on a foreign stock exchange and will be forced to be more transparent about their social and environmental performance (KPMG 2005). However, imitation of Western practices cannot be taken for granted, given that firms from developing economies are often subject to very different domestic pressures. Above all, many oil companies in developing economies are either state-owned or the state has an important interest in them. Many oil companies in developing economies – particularly state-owned oil companies – will not require a foreign stock market listing.

The adoption of better environmental practices by oil companies from developing economies is vital, given that half of the world's known oil and gas reserves are controlled by just five national oil companies from developing nations. Therefore, a crucial limitation of current reporting is that some of the world's more important producers of oil from the Middle East or Asia may decide not to publish Western-style CSR reports and may not conform to international standards such as the 2002 sustainability reporting guidelines of the Global Reporting Initiative or the 2005 Oil and Gas Industry Guidance on Voluntary Sustainability Reporting.

The major national oil companies of the Middle East – where most of the world's oil is located – such as Saudi Aramco and the National Iranian Oil Company – still do not publish CSR or sustainability reports. The notable exception in the Middle East was the Abu Dhabi National Oil Company, which has published annual health, safety and environment reports since 2004. Some of the leading multinational oil companies from developing economies such as Venezuela's PDVSA and Indian Oil – both of which are listed in the *Fortune* magazine ranking of the world's 500 biggest corporations – also do not issue CSR or sustainability reports.

While commenting on the low number of multinational companies that publish CSR reports, Bennett and Burley (2005) asked provocatively: 'In what realm of life other than the strange world of [corporate social responsibility] would a 2–3% take-up rate be considered to be a success?' (Bennett and Burley 2005, reported in Blowfield and Murray 2008, 353). The number of multinational oil and gas companies with a CSR report is probably much higher than 3 per cent (the figure provided by Bennett and Burley for all multinational companies), but the value of environmental reporting will be greatly limited if the majority of oil companies cannot be persuaded to use some commonly agreed indicators.

The lack of an environmental report does not necessarily imply that a company is irresponsible. For instance, it has been acknowledged that Saudi Aramco has responsible environmental protection measures in place. In addition, Saudi Aramco has invested in scientific research into fuel cell technology, carbon sequestration (capturing emitted carbon and storing it) and innovative measures for desulphurising petroleum (Marcel and Mitchell 2005, 158–9). However, without regular publication of consistent environmental data, it will be more difficult to compare the performance of companies and to encourage them towards improvements.

More serious than the publication of environmental reports is the fact that state-owned companies rarely pursue 'green' entrepreneurial opportunities, as we already identified in Chapter 2. Valerie Marcel's book on state-owned oil companies in the Middle East concluded that 'many producers lack an understanding of how they can benefit from proactive action on ... environmental fronts, notably on the climate change regime, emissions trading and energy efficiency programs' (Marcel and Mitchell 2005, 159). In other words, there is relatively little understanding of the win-win outcomes of pursuing environmental improvements and technical innovations in this area. Furthermore, the example of Venezuela's PDVSA in Chapter 2 suggests that a state-owned company may reverse its environmental initiatives as a result of government policy. This raises the importance of appropriate government policy to encourage environmental improvements.

Importance of government regulation

Critics of voluntary CSR initiatives from the NGO community often have an ideological preference for government regulation and legal liability as the desirable alternatives for improving corporate standards of behaviour (Christian Aid 2004; International Council on Human Rights Policy 2002). In contrast to this position, the author of this book believes that we need a clear cost-benefit analysis of regulation or 'hybrid' voluntary–regulatory solutions. Indeed, many developing nations may not have the capacity to effectively regulate a technically sophisticated industry, and voluntary initiatives may offer a better hope of addressing environmental issues. Therefore, our starting point here is simply pragmatic, asking to what extent the intrinsic motivation of companies can replace government regulation as the determinant of responsible corporate behaviour.

The earlier discussion already suggests that companies can carry out many environmental improvements without the need for actual regulation. The oil and gas sector was able to develop its own environmental reporting standards without government involvement (2005 Guidance), specific companies were able to achieve much greater environmental improvements than those prescribed by regulators (for instance, BP's emissions reductions) and government officials often lacked the technical knowledge available to company engineers with regard to the feasibility of improvements to plant and equipment (for instance, replacing steel tubes with chrome tubes). All of these arguments support the case for CSR.

At the same time, the earlier discussion provided evidence that there are limitations on voluntary measures to tackle the environmental challenges, including variability of practices between companies and the lack of environmental improvements by some companies. We should not assume that regulation can effectively address all of the environmental challenges; neither should we expect that voluntary CSR can 'fix' all of the environmental problems. However, there are strong arguments from a business perspective for the need for government regulation in many instances.

Various studies in leading business journals provide evidence that companies gain competitive advantages from environmental

---

Box 4.2: The development of clean burning petrol by ARCO

In 1991, the US Atlantic Richfield Company (ARCO) announced that it had developed a new, cleaner burning petrol using a formula called EC-X. The company added that ARCO would produce this less polluting petrol only if the state of California introduced a law that all petrol sold in the state be produced using the same formula.

The EC-X formula was not unique in the industry, since other oil refiners had also developed cleaner burning petrol formulas. The crucial difference was that the EC-X formula was 'better suited to ARCO's oil refineries and crude oil supply than to ARCO's competitors' resources'. As McWilliams *et al.* (2002) argued, 'ARCO's formula cannot be a source of sustained competitive advantage unless these substitutes are restricted.'

Therefore, legislation by the state of California would have had an uneven impact on ARCO's competitors because it would have raised their costs of legal compliance and would have provided ARCO with a commercial advantage.

Source: McWilliams *et al.* 2002.

---

competences as a result of government regulation, rather than voluntary environmental initiatives. A study by McWilliams *et al.* (2002) found that companies may even lobby for environmental regulations, if these regulations lead to an uneven impact on different companies in the industry by disproportionately raising rivals' costs and thereby improving a firm's overall competitive position. The authors provided an illuminating example from the oil and gas industry: the development of a new formula (EC-X) for cleaner burning petrol by the US company ARCO (see Box 4.2). The study implies that the development of an innovative environmental solution does not guarantee a company superior commercial advantages by itself – if other companies in the same industry are able to develop similar solutions. It is either the uniqueness of the innovation or legislative restrictions that lead to the commercial profitability of the environmental innovation.

Indeed, management thinkers assert that environmental regulations are absolutely essential for innovation, by creating the necessary context for speeding innovation. Van der Linde argued that environmental regulations are vital to pressurise firms to begin the process of environmental innovation, while sending signals to business leaders that environmental issues will be more important in future. According to this view, firms need to be pushed by government because they perceive change and innovation as unsettling and may be reluctant to pursue new environmental strategies on their own account (van der Linde 1993). Michael Porter and Claas van der Linde doubt that voluntary corporate action can replace government regulations:

> The belief that companies will pick up on profitable opportunities without a regulatory push makes a false assumption about competitive reality – namely, that all profitable opportunities for innovation have already been discovered, that all managers have perfect information about them and that organization incentives are aligned with innovating. (Porter and van der Linde 1995, 127)

Porter and van der Linde set out six reasons why environmental regulation is necessary: (1) to create pressure to motivate companies to innovate; (2) to introduce environmental improvements in cases where it is not possible to completely offset the costs of complying with the law; (3) to alert and educate companies about the opportunities for better resource use and technological improvements; (4) to raise the likelihood that product and process innovations in general will be environmentally friendly; (5) to create a demand for environmental improvements until the market is capable of perceiving and measuring the benefits from environmental improvements; and (6) to level the playing field during the transitional period to innovation-based environmental solutions, to ensure that a company cannot gain a competitive advantage by avoiding environmental improvements (Porter and van der Linde 1995, 128).

Various oil company executives interviewed by the author particularly stressed the last point made by Porter and van der Linde: the need for government intervention to ensure a level playing field. One senior executive of a British oil firm pointed out that 'at the moment, there is a skewed playing field', where Western firms may spend more money on social and environmental improvements than their non-Western counterparts, while they may be excluded from certain profitable regions altogether such as the oilfields in Sudan and Burma. Chinese oil companies were typically singled out for criticism over their lack of environmental care and aggressive tactics in entering new countries. While some of the corporate views may be the result of unjustified fears or even prejudice, they demonstrate the real concerns of executives that their companies will incur additional spending while rival companies will gain from not implementing social and environmental measures. Company executives were not clear how a level playing field could be ensured in practice, but there was a shared sense that companies should be rewarded and not penalised for incurring costs for environmental improvements.

There is evidence to support the argument that government action creates pressure to motivate companies to innovate, even among the most forward-thinking companies such as BP. The decision of BP to pioneer the development of carbon trading schemes (see Box 4.1 above) was motivated at least in part by the expectation that governments would regulate greenhouse gas emissions in future. According to the most extensive study on BP's emissions trading system to date, BP's two main goals in introducing the system were (1) 'to gain experience with the policy instrument that was a likely mechanism to be deployed in a future, economy-wide emissions limitation program'; and (2) 'that a successful demonstration of emissions trading would forestall alternative, more costly policy responses such as an emissions tax' (Victor and House 2006). As one former BP manager interviewed commented: 'I can't say what moved John Browne, but we knew that Kyoto was inevitable sooner or later. Being the first company to develop this [emissions trading system] would benefit us in more ways than one.' In other words, BP decided to use the instrument of carbon trading because it knew that regulation was looming and because it wanted to stave off government regulation in the form of government-set standards or a carbon tax.

Indeed, BP's efforts helped towards staving off regulation. The company's experience in carbon trading earned it an advisory role in developing both the UK's emissions trading system and the European Union's Emission Trading Directive (Hoffman 2004). While BP's emission trading system did not lead directly to the development of European trading systems and there were differences in these systems, BP was able to influence the selection of emissions trading as the preferred policy instrument for addressing emissions reductions within Europe. The study by Victor and House (2006) commented:

> BP's experience helped to convince the UK government to deploy a trading system. And BP's European operations will be required to comply with the emerging European emission trading system – itself built partly on the experience with the UK system. In this context, it is unlikely that BP will pursue again its own internal trading system since BUs [business units] must already contend with market signals from the UK and EU systems.   (Victor and House 2006, 2105)

Government intervention can also help to explain the most visible environmental improvement by oil companies, namely the reduction of oil spills caused by tankers since the 1970s, which we discussed earlier. Oil companies and their industry associations typically explain the reduction in oil spills as a result of voluntary measures ranging from ship inspections to the introduction of oil tankers with a double hull. In the words of one oil and gas publication, it was the voluntary actions of companies and their industry associations that 'designed and broadcast numerous means to prevent spills and to enhance preparedness and response to improve the ability to recover spilt oil and mitigate effects from spills' (IPIECA *et al.* 2002). However, such reconstructed historical accounts fail to acknowledge the enormous government pressures that followed oil tanker accidents such as the *Torrey Canyon* oil spill in 1967 and the *Prestige* oil spill in 2002. Indeed, the voluntary oil company initiatives for addressing marine pollution from the late 1960s onwards may not have happened without government pressures (see Box 4.3).

Box 4.3: The development of the regime for addressing marine oil pollution

Following the *Torrey Canyon* oil spill off the British coast in 1967, governments came under massive public pressure to regulate the sea transportation of oil. Eight governments (including the UK Government) approached the predecessor of the International Maritime Organization (IMO) to re-examine the issue of compensation and liability for oil spills. Shipping companies were keenly aware of the public pressure on governments to address marine pollution, and voluntary agreements offered them the chance of influencing international rules before national governments could impose unfavourable rules on them. The Assistant Secretary-General of the IMO narrated the rationale for the new maritime regime:

> There was general agreement on the need for a uniform international regime on liability and compensation for pollution damage resulting from tanker incidents. All the parties involved recognised that the alternative to such an international regime would be a system of unilateral national legislation under which ships, cargoes and insurers might be subjected to different and uncoordinated laws in different countries. This was clearly undesirable for an industry as global as shipping. (Mensah 2004, 45–6)

In other words, voluntary initiatives such as TOVALOP and OPOL (see above) were designed to stave off national regulation. In the process of negotiations with the oil and shipping sectors, a series of specific oil-related international treaties was established that complemented the voluntary oil and gas industry initiatives, including the 1969 International Convention on Civil Liability for Oil Pollution Damage and the 1971 International Convention on the Establishment of an International Fund for Compensation for Oil Pollution Damage, which provided for the liability of an owner of a ship for oil pollution and established a compensation system, and general treaties with application to the oil and gas industry such as the 1973 International Convention on Marine Pollution, which covered oil pollution at sea.

The voluntary measures by companies did not fully achieve the aims of influencing public policy; for instance, companies were unable to prevent the imposition of the principle of 'strict liability' for oil spills. But one tangible consequence of the proactive stance of companies was the international acceptance of a maximum amount of compensation for oil spills irrespective of the actual damage caused, a principle opposed by critics. The 1992 Civil Liability Convention and the 1992 Fund Convention, which amended the earlier international conventions, kept the provision of a maximum amount (the maximum amount of compensation under the 1992 conventions was c. US$190 million). The inadequacy of this provision was revealed in 2003, when the Oil Pollution Compensation Fund admitted that this maximum amount would cover only 15 per cent of the costs of the oil spill caused by the oil tanker *Prestige* the previous year, which led to further calls for regulation.

Sources: Encyclopedia Britannica 2004; International Oil Pollution Compensation Funds 2004.

A crucial problem of relying on government intervention is that some developing economies may not have the capacity to set and enforce basic environmental standards. Indeed, the lack of environmental regulation in developing economies may be the main argument for encouraging voluntary environmental programmes among companies. The author of this book has encountered different examples of such voluntary measures, even when there was little government pressure to do so, for instance, the replacement of old pipelines in Nigeria and the introduction of the European standards of environmental reporting in Egypt. However, while technical solutions of this nature may yield many environmental benefits, managerial choices on fundamental issues such as the level of environmental spending in a joint venture with a state-owned company or the commercial use of natural gas may be dependent on government action.

The example of gas flaring demonstrates the constraints of voluntary initiatives in developing economies. The World Bank calculated that the annual volume of flared and vented gas is about 110 billion cubic metres, which would be sufficient to provide the combined annual natural gas consumption of Germany and France. Voluntary initiatives to reduce gas flaring can potentially lead to a win-win outcome for companies and the environment: selling associated gas can generate earnings for companies while reducing greenhouse gas emissions. The World Bank has encouraged voluntary initiatives and public–private partnerships in order to reduce gas flaring in the oil and gas sector, as part of its Global Initiative on Natural Gas Flaring Reduction (GGFR). However, a 2004 report by GGFR found that 'only a few oil-producing countries have significantly reduced associated gas flaring and venting volumes, and in most jurisdictions flaring and venting volumes continue to rise with increased oil production.' While the World Bank was keen on promoting voluntary initiatives on gas flaring, the report conceded that 'regulation can and should play an important role in achieving reductions in flaring and venting volumes in developing countries' (World Bank 2004, 1–2).

In the case of gas flaring, a crucial constraint of voluntary initiatives is the regulatory environment of the commercial gas markets. To use an extreme example, Nigeria is believed to lose between US$500 million and US$2.5 billion per year as a result of lost revenues from gas flaring. Oil companies have invested billions of dollars in new gas facilities in Nigeria over recent years, partly as a result of tax incentives provided by the government, but a significant part of the associated gas continues to be flared. A report on gas flaring in Nigeria identified 'inappropriate pricing, lack of gas sector policy, and lack of infrastructure for transmission and distribution' as the key problems preventing the commercial use of associated gas (reported in World Bank 2004, 24). In other words, the government failed to provide the necessary conditions for creating an efficient natural gas market. Oil companies are unable to create a functioning market for natural gas without the appropriate regulatory environment such as 'open access rules' to the gas network, which in turn can create market competition.

To sum up, the above discussion suggests that there are significant constraints to voluntary initiatives in the absence of a conducive regulatory environment. This does not imply that we should trust governments to deliver environmental improvements more effectively than companies. Indeed, companies may prove to be more effective and creative in delivering actual environmental improvements than policy makers. But the available evidence suggests that regulation or even the threat of regulation on issues such as oil spill compensation and the use of double-hull ships was undoubtedly the key stimulus for oil companies to improve their environmental record from the 1970s onwards. Many 'voluntary' environmental initiatives in the oil and gas sector might not have happened without government pressures on the oil companies.

Consumption of oil and gas

While some oil companies were successful in achieving environmental improvements, their absolute impact on the industry's environmental footprint remains questionable. A 2005 report by Henderson Global Investors – *Carbon 100* – analysed the carbon emissions of the 100 largest companies listed on the UK stock exchange (the FTSE 100). The report found that the oil and gas sector was responsible for 41 per cent of direct carbon emissions among the FTSE 100 companies, followed by electricity (21 per cent) and mining (13 per cent).

Henderson Global Investors did not concentrate exclusively on direct carbon emissions generated by companies (e.g., emissions from the running of an oil refinery), but also considered indirect emissions generated by consumers (e.g., emissions from petrol used in cars). These 'indirect' carbon emissions are much more significant in the oil and gas sector than direct ones. In its 2003 Sustainability Report, BP admitted that 'emissions from the products we sell are currently about 15 times higher than emissions from our operations'. BP estimated that its products emitted 1,298 million tonnes of greenhouse gases, equivalent to 5 per cent of the world's total emissions from fossil-fuel consumption. Equally, Shell stated in its 2003 Shell Report that '85% of the GHGs [greenhouse gases] from the oil we extract are emitted when it is used in customers' vehicles' (reported in Henderson Global Investors 2005, 12–13).

While other companies unfortunately did not provide equivalent data, it is clear that the oil and gas industry's 'indirect' impact on climate change continues to be crucial, notwithstanding the companies' achievement in meeting their own voluntary targets or their participation in emissions trading schemes. However, while the 2005 Guidance on Voluntary Sustainability Reporting requires oil companies to report on their direct greenhouse gas emissions, it fails to investigate the more significant 'indirect' impact.

The importance of 'indirect' impact raises deeper questions about the social responsibility of companies for the use of the products they sell. Prominent examples include the 'indirect' impact of fast food restaurants on obesity, the 'indirect' impact of tobacco products on citizens' health or, in our case, the impact of oil and gas products on climate change. We do not attempt to apportion the degree of responsibility here but rather highlight the problematic nature of an industry's products. The report by Henderson Global Investors stated: 'While carbon emissions from products should not be attributed to companies in the same way as emissions associated with company operations, the demand for these products is likely to be affected by measures to curb climate change' (Henderson Global Investors 2005, 12).

The importance of 'indirect' impact also raises questions about the role that oil companies play in sustainable development. As Blowfield and Murray (2008, 236) pointed out, 'it is important not to conflate notions of eco-efficiency with those of sustainable development.' On the one hand, eco-efficiency has become a corporate goal for BP and other oil companies. Oil companies can make their refineries and production sites more eco-efficient by using less energy or generating less waste. On the other hand, the harmful nature of oil products contravenes the notion of sustainable development. The use of oil products is simply unsustainable, if judged by the definition of sustainable development as 'meeting the needs of the present generation without compromising the ability of future generations to meet their own needs' (World Commission on Environment and Development 1987). Ultimately, the only way of making oil companies 'sustainable' would be to shift away from the business of oil and gas altogether.

Some oil company executives recognised a long time ago that oil might not always remain the core activity for oil companies. Jeroen van der Veer, the CEO of Shell, stated over ten years ago that 'We work with a finite hydrocarbon resource and want to make sustainable development a reality. The foundation for that is world-class performance of whatever we do' (quoted in Frynas 2003a). In this context, Shell's and BP's expansion into renewable energy in the late 1990s was potentially significant. In 1997, Shell International Renewables (SIR) was created as a new core business alongside such established businesses as oil products and chemicals, while BP created a BP Alternative Energy segment in 2005 (BP Solar had existed since 1998). At the start of the twenty-first century, Shell and BP were among the world's four or five largest solar energy companies, in addition to their expansion into hydrogen, biomass, geothermal energy and wind energy (Frynas 2003a).

However, Shell and BP have since changed their strategy and have scaled down their investments in renewable energy. CEO Jeroen van der Veer recently had a change of heart on renewable energy and, by 2007, Shell had sold off most of its solar business (Macalister 2007). John Browne's successor as CEO of BP – Tony Hayward – also suggested in late 2007 that BP will get back to basics, namely focusing on the core activity of oil and gas production (Brower 2007). Indeed,

Tony Hayward considered selling a part or all of BP's renewable energy unit in early 2008 (Macalister 2008). Even before Tony Hayward succeeded John Browne in 2007, a leading petroleum magazine commented:

> While BP's commitment to alternative energies is beyond doubt, there is no suggestion that alternative-energy schemes will remain anything other than peripheral to its main business of producing oil and gas for decades – especially because technology continues to increase recoverable [oil and gas] reserves and open up new horizons to development. (Nicholls 2007)

Shell and BP decided to reconsider their renewable energy business for commercial reasons. The profits from the renewable energy business were not as high as BP and Shell had previously hoped. Furthermore, the expectations of future revenues from renewable energy were also less optimistic than before. Shell's CEO Jeroen van der Veer specifically highlighted forecasts that even with technological breakthroughs alternative energy sources would only be able to provide about 30 per cent of global energy by the mid-twenty-first century (Macalister 2007).

Ultimately, we cannot expect oil companies to invest in more sustainable alternatives without government regulation and monetary incentives. Indeed, Tony Hayward of BP has called on the world's governments to introduce regulations limiting the amount of carbon dioxide that can be emitted each year and called for subsidies towards the development of renewable energy technologies (Hargreaves 2008). Companies are unlikely to achieve true sustainability by voluntary measures.

Conclusion

This chapter has demonstrated that some companies have made progress on the environmental aspects of their operations. Environmental reporting is improving, new technologies are developed and tangible improvements are made. BP's achievement in reducing greenhouse gas emissions encapsulates the creativity and capacity of oil companies to deal with environmental issues. Judging by the evidence in this chapter, CSR has potential for addressing environmental challenges.

However, we have also outlined the constraints to CSR initiatives. The inadequacies of current environmental reporting undermine efforts to transform the environmental practices of the global oil and gas industry. As long as environmental reporting fails to address actual impacts, the credibility of environmental initiatives will remain limited. Furthermore, the impact of corporate environmentalism is likely to remain severely constrained as long as national oil companies from developing nations fail to engage in environmental improvements. A recent study on national oil companies (NOCs) noted that 'NOCs' investments in countries with ongoing human rights, sustainability, and environmental challenges have complicated international efforts to create a more effective architecture to address rights crises, conflict management over energy resources and environmental stewardship' (Chen 2007, 91).

But even if more NOCs such as Brazil's Petrobras voluntarily engage in environmental improvements, there are clear limitations to voluntarism. As this chapter demonstrates, many crucial environmental issues continue to depend on regulatory guidance and government action will be required to create the right incentives for companies to invest resources in new technologies and environmental improvements such as gas flaring reductions. The earlier example of BP's carbon trading scheme suggests that even CSR pioneers require regulatory pressure to motivate them to innovate. Regulatory pressures are even more important for motivating NOCs, since they are state-owned and act as agents of governments.

More fundamentally, multinational oil companies face a conflict of interest between commercial interests and environmental concerns.

On the one hand, oil and gas deposits are often located near or inside ecologically vulnerable areas in developing economies.

Commercial development carries high risks of environmental damage in these areas, while the lack of commercial development of these areas would mean less profit for oil companies. Not surprisingly, even corporate leaders in 'sustainability' may decide that commercial interests are more important than ecological concerns. Examples include the decision of Petrobras to drill for oil in the Yasuni National Park in Ecuador (Chen 2007) and the construction of the BP–Statoil Baku–Ceyhan pipeline through the catchment area for mineral springs in Georgia (Centre for Civic Initiatives *et al.* 2005). All three companies – Petrobras, BP and Statoil – are considered world-wide 'sustainability' leaders in the oil and gas sector, yet all three companies failed to observe best environmental practices in these projects and disregarded concerns raised by environmentalists and the governments of Ecuador and Georgia.

On the other hand, the consumption of the oil and gas products sold by oil companies is inherently harmful to the environment as a result of carbon emissions. The production and sales of these harmful products remain the core activities for oil companies, and a shift by the oil companies towards alternative energy sources is unlikely in the near future. Indeed, the significance of Shell's and BP's investments in renewable energy may have been overstated. As one NGO report critically remarked in 2002: 'While BP's solar power activities occupy nearly 20% of its communications, they account for just 0.17% of BP's total turnover' (Muttitt and Marriott 2002, 46).

To sum up in a single sentence: CSR can help companies to achieve greater eco-efficiency, but it cannot help them to achieve sustainable development.

FIVE

The development challenge

This chapter evaluates the potential of the current CSR agenda for addressing international development challenges, by focusing on the experience of the oil and gas sector. Both development agencies and companies have in recent years made claims about the positive role that CSR could play in contributing to international development goals such as poverty alleviation and health improvements. As the UK Government's Department for International Development (DfID) argued, 'By following socially responsible practices, the growth generated by the private sector will be more inclusive, equitable and poverty reducing' (Department for International Development 2001, 2, quoted in Jenkins 2005, 525). The contribution of firms to development goals is particularly relevant in developing economies, where the state has often failed to provide basic infrastructure, education and health facilities.

The linking of CSR to international development goals is a hugely significant development, in that firms are not simply expected to act appropriately in terms of responsible environmental practices or health and safety, but also to play an important role in public interventions such as the United Nations Millennium Development Goals (MDGs). If firms are seriously expected to play such a role,

CSR cannot be simply seen from the business perspective, as the expectations of what CSR could potentially accomplish seem to have become much broader. From society's perspective, it is important to assess the contribution that private companies can make to international development goals.

What constitutes 'international development' can, of course, be differently interpreted. In addition to basic human needs, it could encompass broad goals such as income distribution or value creation. The United Nations MDGs include such goals as halving global poverty, reducing child mortality and increasing access to safe drinking water.[1] However, poverty appears to be the key global concern today. Indeed, the UK DfID defines 'international development' in terms of 'efforts to bring people out of poverty'.[2] When we discuss international development goals with reference to private sector initiatives in this chapter, we focus on poverty.

Tackling the development challenge

Since the late 1990s, international organisations such as the World Bank and the United Nations, as well as national development agencies such as the US Agency for International Development (USAID) and the DfID in the UK, have embraced CSR and discussed the role that the private sector can play in achieving development goals including poverty alleviation, education and health improvements (Jenkins 2005). In December 2005, the UN special envoy for HIV/Aids in Africa even proposed that multinational firms should contribute 0.7 per cent of their annual pre-tax earnings to combating HIV/Aids; this figure corresponds to the UN target for developed nations' contribution to development aid as a proportion

---

[1] The United Nations MDG website at www.un.org/millenniumgoals/ (accessed 12 January 2006).
[2] The DfID website at www.dfid.gov.uk/ (accessed 12 January 2006).

of GDP (White and Jack 2005). This is perhaps a somewhat radical opinion, but the expectations placed on the private sector have undoubtedly grown, particularly in countries with Anglo-Saxon business traditions. Most notably, USAID has engaged in multiple partnerships with private firms such as Chevron, Microsoft and IKEA to support and partly fund initiatives ranging from building new homes in Armenia to renewable energy schemes in the Philippines (US Agency for International Development 2003).

A number of Western governments have consciously passed the responsibility for development efforts from the public to the private sector. A striking example was the Consortium for Development and Relief in Angola (CDRA), which comprised NGOs such as Catholic Relief Services, Care and Save the Children. Until 2002, CDRA received funding from government bodies such as USAID to help in the post-war rebuilding efforts in Angola. In 2002, the US Government informed CDRA that the development projects would now be financed by Chevron, not US Government funds, giving the NGOs two weeks to accept the proposed change in funding. One organisation – Catholic Relief Services – refused to accept Chevron money and subsequently faced a US$700,000 funding shortfall as a result, which put its development efforts at risk. But the US Government succeeded in shifting the responsibility for the development efforts from the public to the private sector.

The calls for greater involvement of private firms in human development reflect the growing importance of Foreign Direct Investment (FDI) relative to Official Development Assistance (ODA) to developing countries, with FDI now reportedly outpacing ODA by a factor of three to one (Jenkins 2005, 529). A senior USAID official admitted in an interview with the author that USAID seeks financial contributions from firms because there are 'fewer resource flows to developing countries through ODA'. As a consequence of world-wide liberalisation and deregulation, therefore, firms are now being called upon to go beyond their traditional role of generating economic growth (and thus indirectly helping goals such as poverty alleviation) towards playing a more direct role in alleviating poverty and other development goals.

In a small number of industries, including the oil and gas industry, firms are now making significant contributions towards community development projects such as hospitals, schools and micro-credit schemes. Global spending by oil, gas and mining companies on community development programmes was estimated at over US$500 million per year in 2001 (Wells *et al.* 2001), but the figure is much higher today. The four oil majors – Shell, Exxon, BP and Chevron – spent almost US$500 million between them in 2006 alone.

The biggest spender was Venezuela's PDVSA, which reportedly spent US$13.3 billion on 'social development' in 2006 (this is up from US$6.9 billion in 2005). Other state-owned companies such as Saudi Aramco and Russia's Gazprom have also spent billions of dollars on social investments (see Box 5.1), although exact figures are frequently not available for many of these companies. Among the commercially operating multinational oil companies, the biggest spender was probably the Brazilian oil company Petrobras, which reportedly spent 545 million Brazilian reais (about US$255 million) on 'social investments' in 2006, compared with US$156 million by France's Total, US$140 million by Shell and US$138 million by Exxon (see Table 5.1). Most of the funding was targeted at developing economies, where most oil production takes place and where the development needs are greatest. But a number of Western companies have also made considerable investments in their home country, Exxon notably spending US$79 million on local communities in the United States in 2006 (57 per cent of the company's social investment budget for that year).

Large social investments by companies such as PDVSA, Saudi Aramco and Gazprom reflect the fact that state-owned or partly state-owned companies pursue the social objectives of the government. PDVSA in Venezuela has greatly expanded its social investments since 2002 because President Chavez has directed the company

---

Box 5.1: Social investments by state-owned oil and gas companies

PDVSA is the biggest spender on social investments in the oil and gas sector, disbursing US$13.3 billion in 2006. PDVSA directly supports projects in line with 'national missions' set by the government of Venezuela, which relate to education, access to health services, access to basic food items, agricultural development, skills training for the unemployed, promotion of indigenous communities and, somewhat unusually, provision of identification documents to previously unregistered citizens.

Saudi Aramco has particularly focused on education. The company has built almost 135 schools in Saudi Arabia. Saudi Aramco reportedly plans to spend over US$10 billion on building a new Western-style private university, 'King Abdullah University of Science and Technology', in Saudi Arabia over the coming years. In comparison, Saudi Arabia's total annual education budget is about $15 billion.

Russia's Gazprom's largest recent social investment was a 'gasification' scheme to extend gas provision to 13 million Russians, which required the construction of more than 13,000 kilometres of new distribution gas pipelines over 2005–7. In 2006, Gazprom reportedly spent over 17 billion roubles (over US$650 million) on this scheme alone, which was more than the combined total social spending by Total, Shell, Exxon, BP and Chevron in the same year.

However, a number of state-owned companies spend considerably less on social investment programmes than Saudi Aramco and Gazprom. For instance, Mexico's Pemex reportedly spent over US$100 million on 'cash and non-cash contributions' in 2005. Ninety-five per cent of these financial donations and other contributions (e.g., donations of asphalt) went directly to state and municipal government authorities in Mexico; in effect, the active engagement of Pemex in social investments was much smaller than that by commercial companies such as Exxon, Shell and BP.

Sources: various newspapers, magazines and company websites; social investment spending figures converted from local currency into US dollars, using currency exchange rates from *The Economist* for 31 December of a given year.

TABLE 5.1: *Community investments by selected oil companies in 2006*

Company	Country	2006 spending (US$ million)	Community investment by focus area			
			Community health	Community education	Entrepreneurs / SMEs	Local sourcing
BP	UK	107	+	+	+	+
Shell	UK	140	+	+	+	+
Chevron	USA	91	+	+	+	+
Exxon	USA	138	+	+	+	+
Statoil	Norway	10	+	+	+	+
Norsk Hydro*	Norway	45		+	+	
Total*	France	156	+	+	+	+
ENI*	Italy	98	+	+	+	+
Repsol*	Spain	34	+	+	+	
OMV	Austria	n/a	+	+	+	
CNOOC	China	n/a		+	+	
Sinopec	China	n/a	+	+		
Lukoil	Russia	62	+	+		
Gazprom	Russia	n/a	+	+		
MOL	Hungary	n/a	+	+		
Petrobras*	Brazil	255	+	+	+	+
Petronas	Malaysia	n/a	+	+	+	
PKN Orlen	Poland	n/a	+	+		
PTT	Thailand	n/a	+	+	+	
Sasol	South Africa	n/a	+	+	+	+

Note: * 2006 spending figure converted from local currency into US dollars, using currency exchange rates from *The Economist* for 31 December 2006.

to embark on ambitious development programmes. Similarly, the king of Saudi Arabia has single-handedly directed Saudi Aramco to spend billions of dollars on specific social projects. In Russia, Gazprom's 'gasification' scheme was promoted as a 'social project of national significance' by the Russian Government.

For a number of reasons, the government may assume that the state-owned oil company is better equipped to deliver social development than other government agencies. The government may seek specific technical skills from the company: for instance, Russia's Gazprom is better equipped to deliver gas supplies to households than other government agencies. The government may also assume that the oil company is capable of operating more independently and professionally than other government agencies: for instance, the king of Saudi Arabia chose Saudi Aramco to build a modern Western-style university because of the company's traditional independence from religious institutions in the kingdom (see Box 5.1). Conversely, a number of state-owned companies, such as Algeria's Sonatrach, have reduced their social investment spending over the last two decades because their respective governments feel that other government departments are now in a better position to fulfil various 'national missions' such as developing infrastructure and building hospitals (Marcel and Mitchell 2005, chapter 6).

While there are differences between commercial oil companies and state-owned oil companies, all large oil companies engage in social investments in some form. In effect, oil companies have become quasi-development agencies with a combined total annual budget of billions of dollars, which raises the question of how effectively the money is actually spent.

The author of this book has analysed recent social and environmental reports by twenty companies to ascertain to what extent oil companies fund community development schemes and what specific focus areas they target. The analysis covered reports of the same twenty companies considered in Chapter 4. As we can see from

Table 5.1, every single company supports some sort of 'community development' or 'social investment'.

All twenty companies support education initiatives and eighteen out of twenty companies support health initiatives aimed at local communities (in addition to education or health initiatives for their workers). However, there is a wide variation in the scope of initiatives and the level of integration. The initiatives range from occasional financial donations to schools or hospitals to the construction of new schools and other facilities. Some initiatives appear to have little integration with the company's activities and exhibit few signs of a 'social strategy' (e.g., a single donation to a medical facility), other initiatives exhibit a high level of integration with the company's operations (e.g., skills training that may help local people to find employment in the oil and gas industry). Among emerging market companies, South Africa's Sasol and Brazil's Petrobras appear to have much more sophisticated and integrated development programmes than, for instance, China's Sinopec or Hungary's MOL.

Some companies go beyond supporting particular health or education projects by attempting to foster the long-term social and economic development of their local communities. This is particularly evident in initiatives to support income-generating projects. On the one hand, companies provide skills training and advice to local entrepreneurs and small and medium enterprises (SMEs), which in turn can generate local income and jobs. Indeed, all ten companies from developed economies support such initiatives, and half of the companies from emerging economies do so. On the other hand, some companies actively pursue 'local sourcing', which means increasing the purchase of local products for their operations (from foodstuffs to oil equipment). Seven out of ten companies from developed economies and two emerging market companies had a policy on increasing local inputs, although some of these policies were the result of legal requirements enforced by host governments. Examples include Sasol's partnership with an NGO to train bird guides for the developing ecotourism industry, Shell's assistance for Indian farmers to gain organic certification, business support centres to help smaller companies to obtain business contracts from oil companies and training programmes in entrepreneurial and marketing skills. A number of companies go beyond social and local economic issues and also see a role for improving the quality of governance in the countries where they operate (see Chapter 6).

However, while there is a wealth of community initiatives, the current reporting on these activities is very weak. The social and environmental reports contain only input and no output measures for their social investment. In other words, companies provide information on how much they have spent on education or philanthropic activities or how many local stakeholders participated in a project, but they provide no measures of how effectively the money was spent. Not even the level of spending is comparable between companies, because it is not clear what is included and what is not (e.g., Exxon's figure includes PR-related donations to arts institutions and spending on public policy research). Not a single company systematically measures the effectiveness of its development interventions, either in terms of scientific measures (e.g., changes in health indicators related to health spending) or in terms of a value-for-money analysis. Oil companies seem to be simply satisfied that they spend money on 'development'. We do not know, therefore, to what extent the community investment has actually yielded tangible benefits for stakeholders.

The development impact is obviously inherently difficult to measure, but it is not impossible to introduce indicators. Most notably, Shell introduced the measure of 'estimated spend on goods and services from locally owned companies' in lower-income countries. However, this example is almost unique in current reporting, and the other companies do not even specify any developmental indicators. Neither does Shell's or any other indicator allow us to assess the actual impact of development interventions or to compare performance between different initiatives and different companies.

A number of companies, including Total, Repsol and Petrobras, have announced that they are producing suitable development indicators. Indeed, companies already use some development indicators at the operational level. Shell uses various development indicators such as 'the repayment rate of loans' in micro-credit schemes for rural communities in Nigeria. Chevron calculates the 'average income of farmers' and the 'number of hectares that were formerly unproductive and are now in use' as measures of success for an agricultural business programme that the company funded in the Philippines. Therefore, we will probably see improvements in social reporting in future.

For the time being, company reports reveal a marked imbalance between environmental and social reporting. On the one hand, environmental reports include a variety of scientific measures of success (carbon dioxide emissions, quantity of oil spills, etc.), as we have seen in Chapter 4. On the other hand, social reports narrate selective examples (or 'stories') of community investment programmes without reference to any measure of success. The reader can either trust these stories or not trust them, but the reader cannot verify or compare the achievements of companies.

Needless to say, community investments can be highly beneficial for stakeholders in the absence of externally verified measures of success, and one could point to various examples of success, including Shell's micro-credit schemes in Nigeria and Chevron's agricultural initiative in the Philippines. One must also remember that the beneficiaries of oil-company-funded projects often have no alternative sources of support, particularly in developing economies where the government has failed in its development role.

Initiatives funded by oil companies gain further credibility because they can draw on international development expertise in many of their funded projects. Indeed, various companies participate in partnerships with established development agencies such as USAID and UNDP, while using NGOs to implement development projects on

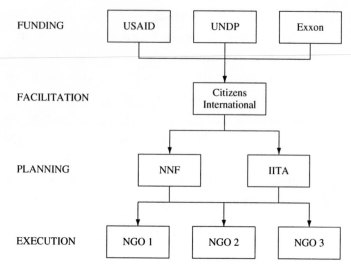

Figure 5.1: Layers of an Exxon-funded agricultural development project in Nigeria

the ground. Figure 5.1 provides the example of an agricultural local community development project, which was partly funded by Exxon in Nigeria. The project was facilitated and planned by a specialist US-based consulting firm called Citizens International, the Africa-based International Institute of Tropical Agriculture (IITA) and the not-for-profit New Nigeria Foundation (NNF), and it was entirely implemented by small indigenous non-governmental organisations. In many instances, multinational companies such as Exxon and Shell use the expertise of development agencies and specialist international development consulting firms such as Citizens International and Chemonics to design suitable development projects, while they use international development specialists, existing medical and educational bodies and NGOs to implement company-funded projects on the ground. Private contractors may even carry out many vital tasks during the preparation of a project, such as carrying out social impact assessment studies, drawing up lists of stakeholders to be consulted or setting the agenda for project funding; a successful example was BP's

Tangguh liquefied natural gas project in Indonesia, which benefited from the specialist expertise of the consulting firm Chemonics. Therefore, the design and implementation of company-funded projects has become more professional over the years.

The professionalisation of community investment is reflected in the restructuring of community relations within oil companies. As one example known to the author, Shell in Nigeria reorganised its community development unit into the Sustainable Community Development (SCD) unit in 2004, with a new emphasis on sustainability and the long-term perspective for all its community development projects. The company has moved away from its focus on infrastructure projects, such as hospitals, towards more promising smaller projects such as micro-credit schemes. The SCD unit hired consultants and development specialists (including a former senior UNDP official and former NGO staff), while entering into partnerships with external development agencies and various NGOs. The unit has also introduced a number of guidelines for implementing development-related projects and some measurement techniques to ensure some consistency. To sum up, the delivery of 'community development' by companies is evolving and becoming increasingly sophisticated. The Akassa community development project in Nigeria is an example of the best development practice that has benefited from a more professional approach by oil companies to development issues (see Box 5.2).

However, a previous study by the author funded by the Nuffield Foundation suggests that, for all the money that oil companies have spent on development initiatives, there are surprisingly few tangible benefits for local stakeholders. Indeed, it is significant that some of the most scathing criticisms of CSR – or rather the community development interventions – were expressed in conversations with the author by former and current oil company staff and company consultants with first-hand experience of CSR practice in the oil and gas sector. Comments by industry insiders

Box 5.2: The Akassa project in Nigeria

Statoil's funding for the Akassa project in south-eastern Nigeria has come to symbolise the potential positive benefits of oil company development interventions and has recently served as a role model for other oil companies and external donors in the Niger Delta.

The Akassa project in Nigeria's Bayelsa State was funded by Statoil (and initially also BP, now Chevron) but was implemented by a development NGO called ProNatura, which had exceptional development expertise and was able to execute the project without interference from oil company managers.

In contrast to most other oil-company-funded projects, the Akassa project was entirely grassroots-based. Rather than outsiders deciding on which specific initiatives should be implemented, the Akassa project was largely driven by the local people. In contrast to the often superficial consultation exercises with local people carried out by oil companies, ProNatura conducted an in-depth appraisal of the needs of the community over a longer period of time in which ProNatura staff went to live in the villages and had extensive discussions with the local people about their problems and the causes of these problems, before even starting to plan any initiatives. The project was fully community-led, involving not just the chiefs (as oil companies had previously done) but the whole community in the planning process, including women and youths. Also, crucially, ProNatura helped to build up the capacity of the local people to help themselves by, among other things, helping to set up new institutions such as a development foundation and community development councils, while providing training and advice to the local people.

In contrast to other oil company projects, the Akassa project was part of a large development plan for the entire Akassa clan (encompassing some 30,000 people in many different villages) rather than focusing on one or several host communities.

The Akassa project has now come to be seen as a benchmark for best practice in the Niger Delta and ProNatura is currently trying to emulate this approach in the process of executing development projects on behalf of France's Total and the tiny oil firm Nexen. But oil company staff in other companies such as Shell and some development professionals have doubts as to whether the Akassa project could be replicated elsewhere in Nigeria or in oil-producing areas in other countries, since there is little impact of oil operations in the Akassa area, where oil operations are located offshore. Statoil started funding the project even before it moved in (and Statoil has not yet started oil production), and the area has enjoyed a long period of peace and stability. As a consequence, ProNatura is said to have faced fewer constraints such as the influence of the dependency mentality. However, one should welcome a success story which could be used as a role model elsewhere.

Sources: interviews in Nigeria and Knight *et al.* 2000.

included: 'CSR is a waste of time', 'CSR is about managing perceptions and making people inside and outside the company feel good about themselves' and 'CSR is a red herring in terms of development projects'. Of course, oil companies have many CSR advocates, who would undoubtedly like to dismiss such claims. But criticism by industry insiders must be taken seriously and calls for an assessment of CSR practice. Accordingly, the rest of the chapter will present the findings of the author's Nuffield Foundation study.

The limitations of community development initiatives

The author has conducted an extensive twelve-month research project on oil-company-funded community development projects in the Gulf of Guinea region, generously funded by the Nuffield Foundation. Eighty-nine interviews were conducted for this research with oil company staff, consultants, NGO staff, local communities, government officials and others in the United Kingdom, the United States, Nigeria, Cameroon and Equatorial Guinea. The study found that the positive effects of company initiatives for local communities were severely constrained by the companies' own motives for community development work, on the one hand, and by various implementation problems, on the other.

Motives for community engagement and their constraints

The Nuffield Foundation study identified four important drivers for firms to embark on community development projects:

- obtaining competitive advantages
- maintaining a 'licence to operate'
- managing external perceptions
- keeping employees happy.

The above list of four motives/drivers is by no means exhaustive and other drivers may be added. Furthermore, social initiatives may also serve to address several of these motives simultaneously or may be partly motivated by a genuine desire 'to do the right thing'. But the list can help to understand why social initiatives have only limited development potential. We shall briefly outline those four drivers and suggest why the companies' motives for embarking on community development projects limit their development benefits.

Obtaining competitive advantages

Companies are sometimes motivated by the desire to obtain a competitive advantage vis-à-vis rival companies with less social engagement. Indeed, in a number of oil-producing countries, socially responsive oil companies appear to have been favoured by the government in the award of oil and gas concessions – although technical, commercial and political motives probably still played the most important role in selecting companies.

For instance, oil companies in Angola have been actively encouraged by the government to contribute towards 'social development' initiatives for a long time, including the Social Bonus Fund of the Angolan state oil corporation, Sonangol, and the Angolan president's Eduardo dos Santos Foundation. One academic writer commented that corporate contributions to the president's foundation – and, by implication, other social initiatives – offered a double advantage to foreign firms of 'being close to the source of power while also making a display of charity' (Messiant 2001). Interviews suggest that, notably, Chevron in Angola has strategically used its social investments in its attempt to renew its stake in Block 0, Angola's most prized oil asset, with an output of 400,000 barrels per day. Even some Chevron staff admitted in private that the announcement of a US$50 million partnership between Chevron, USAID and UNDP in November 2002 was timed to coincide with the Block 0 negotiations. In early 2004, Chevron's concession was finally extended from 2010 to 2030, and the company pledged a further US$80 million to a social fund. In other words, social engagement helped the company to obtain a competitive advantage.

While Chevron's partnership with USAID and UNDP has had discernible development benefits in Angola, there has been controversy with regard to oil companies' payments to the Social Bonus Fund and the president's social foundation. Indeed, it has been suggested that the corporate 'social investment' often served as simply another means of channelling money to Angolan government officials with few development benefits (Frynas and Wood 2001). Beyond the award of concessions, oil companies have occasionally initiated specific social projects to curry favour with a specific government official, for instance through building an orphanage in the official's village or region of origin.

From the perspective of oil companies, the benefit of social initiatives may be to bring managers closer to political decision-makers, while appearing to be socially responsible. From the perspective of broader society, a crucial pitfall of using social initiatives as a competitive weapon is that the development priorities pursued by oil companies may be those of specific government officials and not necessarily those of the supposed beneficiaries of such initiatives.

Maintaining a 'licence to operate'

Firms embark on social investments in order to maintain a 'licence to operate', which means community development projects are initiated as a way of maintaining a stable working environment. In extreme cases such as Nigeria and Colombia, violent conflicts have occasionally halted oil operations, hence oil companies were unable to carry out normal oil production activities without engaging in community development initiatives and essentially buying the local communities' support.

For instance, oil companies in Nigeria have pursued community development initiatives in order to ensure the smooth construction of pipelines, an approach described by one oil sector consultant as the 'rapid construction – zero interruption' approach. Indeed, Shell's main Nigerian affiliate, Shell Petroleum Development Company (SPDC), provided its major contracts managers with a development budget; when a new pipeline was built, the manager was able to initiate a new development project within a community in order for pipeline construction to continue unhindered. When the SPDC team finished the construction of a particular section of the pipeline, the community development budget for the area was simply closed, which followed the firm's logic for embarking on the project in the first instance. Furthermore, one problem of such an approach is that the major contracts managers are not development specialists, and projects are driven by short-term expediencies rather than the long-term development needs of a community. In one extreme case narrated by a Shell manager, SPDC built three town halls in one Nigerian community in the process of building a pipeline, because three community leaders wanted to benefit personally from construction contracts.

If social projects are initiated in order to temporarily buy peace, the companies are unlikely to properly consult the entire affected community. In line with predictions of stakeholder theory (see Chapter 2), firms will listen primarily to those stakeholders who pose the greatest threat to their operations, not those best placed to contribute towards development aims.

Managing external perceptions

Companies also initiate social investments in order to manage external perceptions. Many social initiatives have been started following bad publicity and can be seen as an attempt to improve a company's reputation. For instance, in the village of Okoroba in Bayelsa State, Nigeria, visited by the author years ago, a Shell contractor destroyed a hospital building. Shell promised to build a new hospital but the construction stalled for many years. The hospital was eventually rebuilt by Shell following bad publicity, generated notably by a director of Environmental Rights Action/Friends of the Earth Nigeria, who originated from the village.

Of all the companies studied by the author, the Hungarian company MOL was the most honest in defining the aims of the company's 'social investments':

> Sponsoring activities, in line with our business strategy, send out positive messages and support the achievement of marketing objectives. They also strengthen MOL Group's business position and value and increase its social recognition and as a result earn the respect of society. (MOL Group 2007, 89)

In many other cases, corporate social initiatives have been used for public relations (PR) purposes, notwithstanding their success in fostering the long-term development of a local community. In extreme cases, oil companies have publicised projects which did not exist on the ground or were only partially functional, a practice made easier in developing countries, where it may be difficult to verify such claims. For instance, Shell in Nigeria claimed in an advertising brochure in August 1996 that the Kolo Creek flowstation was providing associated gas for a rural electrification scheme; during the author's visit to the site in early 1997, associated gas was still being flared there.

Kolo Creek is an extreme example of a marketing distortion, but it underlines the importance of PR for CSR practice. If PR priorities precede development priorities, this is likely to affect the planning and the implementation of CSR initiatives. PR needs may, for instance, prioritise media-friendly projects such as donating medical equipment or helping to construct a new hospital, rather than patient local capacity-building or the training of village nurses, which was exactly the lesson of past projects in Nigeria's oil-producing areas. In the words of one oil and gas sector insider: 'amateurism the way that things are done is beyond belief, for example, the way the projects are chosen, until I understood that this was tokenism, it was about managing perceptions [sic].' There is a real danger that PR priorities may constrain development efforts.

Keeping employees happy

While there are important corporate motives for ensuring that external actors have a positive view of the company (governments, local communities, NGOs and the public), companies have compelling internal motives for CSR. Field research for the Nuffield Foundation study suggests that CSR is often driven by the firms' desire to demonstrate to their own employees that the company is a positive force for development. The public criticism of oil and gas companies has had a demoralising effect on oil company staff, with publicised stories of environmental damage, the role of oil in conflicts or arguments that the oil revenues harm local economic development. In particular, expatriate staff in developing countries may feel demoralised when they see how oil riches fail to benefit larger society while enriching the country's elite. In extreme cases, the recruitment of new graduates and the retention of existing staff have been affected. In the words of one oil and gas sector insider: 'You can't stop CSR, because you would demotivate your own employees.'

However, using community development initiatives as a motivational tool is in itself a limiting factor, since the very existence of such initiatives (rather than the long-term development benefit) is a goal in itself for companies. Charitable donations to an orphanage or a school, for instance, may already make staff feel better about themselves, without the need for the firm to ensure the actual development benefits of such work. This may explain the earlier observation that corporate reports do not provide any indicators of how effectively the community development funds are spent.

As social initiatives are, to some extent, driven by what makes staff feel better about themselves, the development priorities may reflect those of the people inside the firm rather than the local community. In one case narrated to the author by a consultant, an American manager from a cattle-farming community in Nebraska initiated a cattle-raising scheme for a local community. It is not that a community could not benefit from a cattle-raising scheme, but rather that such projects are driven by the priorities of individual employees rather than those of local communities.

Pitfalls of the business case

The four subsections above demonstrate that the 'business case for CSR' (that is, the use of social initiatives for attaining corporate objectives) sets limits on what such initiatives can achieve for broader society. Since the 'business case' drives CSR, it is not surprising that many corporate social initiatives do not go beyond narrowly philanthropic gestures like donating objects to local communities such as schoolbooks, mosquito nets or life jackets, without any attempt to consult the community or development specialists. Even such simple gestures sometimes end up as failures. In Equatorial Guinea, Exxon donated mosquito nets to the health ministry for malaria prevention, but the ministry then reportedly sold the nets, not least through export to Cameroon. In Angola, BP reportedly distributed Asian-made condoms as part of an Aids campaign, but the condoms turned out to be too small for African men. In Nigeria, the author witnessed many non-functioning white elephants, including unfinished buildings designed to be health clinics or schools, water projects where water is unfit for consumption or projects such as health clinics which lack lighting, running water, basic equipment or staff.

Since delivering development is not a primary motive for companies to engage in social initiatives, the business case frequently leads to the failure of projects such as the construction of health clinics. According to a leaked 2001 independent audit commissioned by Shell, less than one third of Shell's development projects in Nigeria were fully successful in the sense that they were functional (Anonymous 2001). The audit found that Shell was still essentially trying to buy off the local people with gifts rather than trying to offer them genuine development, which followed the logic of using CSR for maintaining a stable working environment and improving perceptions about Shell. For example, while Shell's SCD unit in Nigeria has been ahead of other oil companies in terms of its development approaches and professionalism, major flaws in its development work remain, and the results of Shell's development work are likely to remain disappointing. Even a number of senior Shell staff and consultants have admitted in private conversations that the creation of the SCD unit is unlikely to have a major impact on the company's behaviour in local communities.

Implementation problems

In addition to the constraints of the business case, the Nuffield Foundation study identified a number of important constraints in the implementation of CSR:

• country- and context-specific issues
• failure to involve the beneficiaries of CSR
• lack of human resources
• social attitudes of oil company staff/focus on technical and managerial solutions
• no integration into a larger development plan.

This list is not exhaustive, but it can serve to point out the limited development potential of CSR initiatives. We shall briefly outline these constraints and suggest why the development benefits are inherently limited.

Country-specific/context-specific issues

Operating in specific countries or contexts may make it difficult for firms to implement even the best CSR ideas. In countries as diverse as Nigeria, Colombia or Yemen, CSR work may also be seriously impeded by conflict (e.g., a guerrilla war or inter-ethnic conflict). Sometimes oil companies have contributed to a conflict, while on other occasions they may be affected by existing conflicts. In either case, a conflict can render oil operations – and notably community relations – particularly challenging. In Nigeria, Chevron's community development projects in Delta State had to stop completely because of inter-ethnic fighting in 2003 and did not resume for at least a year.

Corruption can also prove to be a major obstacle. The author has encountered various oil-company-funded development initiatives which failed as a result of corruption; examples include flawed stakeholder consultation as a result of fraud by a company's community liaison officers, buildings that were not completed as a result of failures by contractors and a micro-credit scheme that collapsed as a result of fraud by those in charge.

The example of Shell in Nigeria demonstrates some of these problems. While Shell's SCD unit has some excellent development strategies and skilful staff, the company also faces many practical implementation problems. SPDC's Nigerian subsidiary, SPDC, suffered from corruption: for example, funds allocated for local communities were on some occasions kept by Shell's community liaison officers, with the collusion of corrupt village chiefs. SPDC also suffered from internal implementation problems as a result of its size and internal company procedures. SPDC's internal company structure was cumbersome, and different arms of the organisation (the SCD unit, the company's area managers and its major project managers) conducted development work without much co-ordination.

Community development may suffer as a result of local factors that are independent of companies, and there is relatively little that a single company can do about corruption or conflict. However, country- and context-specific problems notwithstanding, there are more fundamental limitations to the efficacy of CSR work, such as the failure to involve the beneficiaries of CSR.

Failure to involve the beneficiaries of CSR

Participation and self-help are regarded as the best routes for development assistance by organisations as diverse as the World Bank and Oxfam. A central idea expressed in the World Bank's Comprehensive Development Framework is that the 'doer' (a person, a community, a country, etc.) needs to be 'in the driver's seat' and actively help itself (Ellerman 2001). To quote E. F. Schumacher: '[If] the rural people of the developing countries are helped to help themselves, I have no doubt that a genuine development will ensue … [But it] cannot be "produced" by skilful grafting operations carried out by foreign technicians or an indigenous elite that has lost contact with the ordinary people' (Schumacher 1973, 204–5).

In contrast to best development practice advocated by the World Bank and other development institutions, CSR initiatives have often been conceived by the 'helpers' in the air-conditioned offices of oil companies and consultancies rather than through ongoing participation with the beneficiaries, an approach which follows the logic of CSR serving corporate objectives. An oil company contractor suggested to the author that the failure of some projects was due to the lack of initial consultation and 'emphasis on construction rather than people'. As one example of the failure to consult the local people, a quay was built by an oil company in one riverine village in Nigeria but it was unsuitable for the canoes used by the local people.

Where oil companies have consulted local communities, the consultation exercises have often been superficial and grossly inadequate. In villages visited by the author in West Africa, the local people sometimes saw an oil company representative less than once a year, even in villages where the local community had signed a formal memorandum of understanding with an oil company for the delivery of a range of development projects. When oil company representatives do visit local communities, they do not stay overnight and their consultation exercise may involve only one or several meetings with the key community representatives. In the words of one development professional: 'No one is happy to stay in the village, so they [oil companies] do quick PRAs [participatory rural appraisals] to put it on paper [rather than staying overnight in the village].' The author's research suggests that such brief encounters usually result in the local people spontaneously demanding obvious amenities such as electricity, a school or a hospital, without proper consideration of the economic cost, the local needs, the impact of such schemes or the causes of the community's problems. Oil companies usually fail to consult more broadly beyond local chiefs and community leaders.

The involvement of the beneficiaries of CSR in implementing projects tends to be limited or non-existent, and it may be limited at best to awarding contracts to locally based companies. While the involvement of locally based companies can be beneficial, as it creates local employment, the author's conclusions from experiences in Africa are that these companies are often linked to local strongmen, and the award of contracts simply serves to maintain a stable working environment. The reason that Shell built three town halls in one village (see above) was that three different local chiefs reportedly asked for three construction contracts for themselves and Shell duly complied, while ordinary members of the community were not involved. Such an approach to initiating projects inherently limits the benefits of any potential development schemes.

Worse still, the failure to involve the local people has fostered a dependency mentality. Since the development projects do not genuinely involve the local people, they are seen as 'gifts' from outsiders, and the local people do not feel that they 'own' the projects. Therefore, a given scheme cannot remain functional without the continued support of outsiders, which contravenes a basic principle of development. When the author visited one village and found that the drainage system had broken down, he was told that 'We are appealing to Shell [who built the system] to come do it [sic].' This dependency mentality is aggravated by a widespread belief in many oil-producing countries that oil is part of the people's heritage, and that the local population can expect to share in this wealth. Even the 'best' development projects such as micro-credit schemes can suffer from this mentality; one NGO funded by a gas company claimed that the repayment rate for their micro-credit schemes in the Niger Delta was 86 per cent, while their average repayment rate in Nigeria as a whole was 95 per cent, and that this disparity was ascribed to the 'mentality that they [the local people] deserve it and shouldn't repay'. But even if the local people have the will to fix their drainage system or run another project imposed from outside by themselves, they may not have the right skills or tools to do so, since most projects will not have been designed to use local resources and to be run by the local people themselves once external assistance has dried up.

Many of these problems could be avoided through in-depth consultation and the participation of the local people in genuine self-help initiatives using local knowledge, skills and tools. But the involvement of local communities is inherently constrained by the companies' lack of human resources and the technical/managerial approaches of oil company staff.

Lack of human resources

There are undoubtedly some highly competent staff in oil companies with prior experience in international development issues. As mentioned earlier, companies also use third parties such as consultancy firms and NGOs to help them design and implement community development projects. However, despite the professionalisation of such projects, multinational companies still tend to lack the human resources to plan and execute genuine long-term development schemes.

Few people with international development expertise move into companies, and community development units are often staffed with managers, former administration staff, engineers or former government officials. The lack of a 'career path' for community development specialists inside companies further limits the potential of developing expertise. In one instance narrated to the author, a pipeline manager who reached the top of his salary scale was promoted to the company's community development unit, even though he had no community development expertise. Indeed, the international development training of company staff in community development units is often rudimentary. When BP initiated courses to teach BP managers about issues such as biodiversity and global warming, they typically turned to a business school (the Judge Management Institute at the University of Cambridge) rather than a development institution.

Internal workings of oil companies also render long-term development initiatives more difficult. Asset managers are often rotated between subsidiaries in different countries (e.g., every four years in BP), so they tend to lack a long-term commitment to the local communities where the firm operates. Even if one asset manager has commitment to genuine CSR, his/her successor may not be as committed, and a social initiative may simply be halted by the successor. The championing of development projects with a long-term planning horizon therefore may often depend on the leadership of individual managers, whose term of office is inherently limited. Furthermore, managers often spend very little time in the field and lack an understanding of specific local problems.

To sum up, the lack of systematic human resource processes for the training, appraisal and progression of community development staff limits the effectiveness of community development units, while senior managers may have few personal incentives to maximise the long-term development benefits to local communities. Even if a company has a specialised community development or community relations unit, the rest of the company (such as the major contracts managers, who conduct company operations in rural areas) operates according to 'business as usual', with little regard for long-term development needs.

Social attitudes of oil company staff

Related to the lack of human resources, CSR initiatives are inherently flawed as a result of the social attitudes of oil company staff, which means the social values that guide decisions made by company staff.

The people in charge within oil companies (i.e., the company directors, asset managers, etc.) usually have a managerial and/or engineering background. They are highly capable of dealing with technical and managerial challenges, which is reflected in their approaches to CSR. As Michael Blowfield argued: 'The technologies used in CSR reflect a preference for measurement, quantitative data-processing and particular means of communication … segmenting information into quantifiable components to aid the process of management' (Blowfield 2005, 522). This preference can help to explain both the success of many environmental initiatives and the failure of many social initiatives. When the corporate will is present and the CSR challenge can be reduced to distinct quantifiable technical and managerial tasks, oil companies can perform CSR tasks to a high standard. As discussed in Chapter 4, BP's mission to reduce carbon dioxide emissions, led by the company's CEO, John Browne, was very successful. A technical/managerial challenge such as carbon dioxide emissions can be reduced to 'metrics', 'indicators' or 'guidelines' and job performance can be quantified. Therefore, technical/managerial approaches can successfully address environmental challenges, but they are often insufficient in addressing complex social problems where soft skills, patience and interpersonal skills are much more important.

The limitations of technical/managerial approaches can be seen in the manner in which local communities are consulted. A consultation exercise is inherently qualitative and inherently discursive requiring in-depth discussions and the building of a good rapport with people. Treating consultation from a technical/managerial perspective leads managers to speed up discussions with local communities and to try to achieve an immediate goal (such as a written list of local demands) rather than trying to build bridges with the local people and spending lengthy periods discussing the causes of problems. In the words of one development professional in Nigeria: 'Shell learned fast new approaches and paid lip service but corrupted the practice, for example, PRAs [participatory rural appraisals] done in two days like an engineering exercise.' This mindset helps to explain the companies' failure to involve the beneficiaries of CSR.

No integration into a larger development plan
Given the importance of the business case and the practical problems of executing CSR schemes, it is perhaps not surprising that corporate social initiatives rarely form part of larger regional development plans. In conducting the Nuffield Foundation study, the author did not encounter a single example of a broad-based collaboration between oil companies on issues such as health, education or enterprise development. This finding is supported by a previous study on multinational oil companies in Azerbaijan and Kazakhstan, which pointed to the limited potential of collective action on development initiatives. The study concluded:

> Quite clearly, getting the companies to work together on projects of which the benefits may not be proportional to their costs is hard, particularly in projects with a combination of problem solving, social well being, company PR and goodwill issues at stake. So even if joining forces would produce stronger and more comprehensive programmes, the unlikely hope of individual benefits puts an effective brake on such efforts. (Gulbrandsen and Moe 2005, 9)

By not integrating CSR or 'social investment' into larger development plans, the development potential of corporate initiatives is greatly limited and resources may not be channelled for the most effective development use. Since projects are often planned to suit short-term expediencies, 'decisions are taken at too low a level as to which projects to execute', as one development professional put it. So there may be little co-ordination in deciding which areas should benefit and how projects can contribute to a greater whole.

Without a larger development plan, a new hospital may not necessarily be built where it is most needed or the value of entrepreneurship training may be severely hampered if it is not accompanied by improved education, improved access to credit, improved communications or access to markets. For instance, one company built a fish-processing plant in Nigeria, which was situated a long distance from trade markets, lacked electricity for cold storage and lacked suitably qualified personnel. As another extreme example, an oil company in Nigeria built a road which ran parallel to another road built by the Niger Delta Development Commission. These are severe examples of co-ordination failures, but they underline the importance of wider planning and co-ordination for the success of development projects.

Worse still, by not integrating CSR into macro-level development plans, oil companies run the risk of causing local conflicts and creating negative development consequences. One example from Nigeria is the concept of a 'host community', namely that oil companies have a social responsibility towards the local community located closest to their oil facilities. Preference for one community may breed jealousy in other communities and inter-communal conflicts. In one extreme case narrated to the author, members of one community burned down houses in a relatively successful 'host community' (which was located closer to oil company premises than their own community) in order to benefit from host community status themselves. This is perhaps the most extreme and terrifying example of how adopting a micro lens rather than a macro lens within CSR can have perilous effects.

Conclusion

This chapter has demonstrated that corporate initiatives have rela-tively little potential for tackling the development challenge. While the professionalisation of community development initiatives is undoubtedly increasing, this chapter questioned recent claims about the positive contribution of CSR to international development. The inescapable conclusion of the chapter is that CSR or 'social invest-ment' in its current form has limited potential for fostering genuine local community development in practice.

At this point, it may be useful to clarify what this chapter does not argue. This chapter does not argue that CSR or 'social investment' is discredited because some corporate initiatives have failed. Development agencies and NGOs also have their share of failed development projects, despite having superior development exper-tise. Development agencies and NGOs can also cause long-term problems for recipient countries: like petrodollars, the influx of public aid is said to create negative 'resource curse' effects (Younger 1992) (see Chapter 6), while aid delivery has come to rely on NGOs, private contractors and others, which can erode governance structures (OECD 2000). Therefore, the issue is not that multinational firms simply make mistakes or create negative externalities. Rather, there are fundamental problems about the capacity of private firms to actively implement development projects and the aspiration of achieving broader development goals through CSR may be flawed.

The Nuffield Foundation study conducted by the author reveals that a key constraint to CSR's role in development is the business case, that is, the subservience of any CSR schemes to corporate objectives. This chapter does not question the companies' right to make profit, but it suggests that profit-maximising motives are often incompatible with good development practice. Given that oil companies are not development agencies, they do not tend to prioritise overall development goals, and there are inherent

limitations to how corporate social initiatives can address the concerns of the local communities.

Furthermore, this chapter has identified a number of practical
constraints to the implementation of successful community development schemes including country- and context-specific issues; the
failure to involve the beneficiaries of CSR; the lack of human resources; technical/managerial approaches of oil company staff; and the
lack of CSR's integration into larger development plans.

Despite all of these constraints, some of the money spent on 'social
investment' does reach the intended beneficiaries, and there are
notable examples of best practice, such as the Akassa project discussed earlier. In the case of Statoil's Akassa project in Nigeria and
BP's Tangguh liquefied natural gas project in Indonesia, interviews
with company insiders point to three factors that can explain the
success of those two initiatives: (1) the company's level of commitment to the local communities went far beyond the business case; (2)
the quality of consultations with the local stakeholders; and (3) the
high quality of staff working for the company. However, the Nuffield
Foundation study found that the Akassa project was exceptional in a
number of respects (see Box 5.2). Similarly, interviews suggest that
the Tangguh project was exceptional, not least because BP's CEO
John Browne took a personal interest in Indonesia and some of BP's
best staff were sent to work on the project. In contrast, the vast
majority of company-funded projects are considered to be much less
successful in terms of development benefits.

Even if companies were able to maximise the development benefits
from their community initiatives, the development benefits from
such efforts will always be limited compared with other economic
contributions that companies make. As companies themselves realise, their main contribution to development is through paying taxes
to governments and supplying energy, as well as providing jobs and
investment. The local community spending is very small compared
with the taxes that companies pay. For instance, Shell reportedly paid

US$17 billion in corporate taxes and collected US$71 billion in excise duties and sales taxes on behalf of governments in 2006, compared with US$140 million spent on 'social investment'. In other words, the host governments received US$88 billion from Shell in 2006 alone, which they could in turn spend on social investment. By implication, much more attention needs to be paid to the quality of spending of petroleum revenues. In the words of a senior World Bank official: 'CSR is missing the boat, the real issues are the fiscal issues ... oil companies have a role to play in the improved management of revenues.' In other words, the crucial challenge for the oil and gas sector is related to governance, which we discuss in the next chapter.

SIX

The governance challenge

This chapter evaluates the potential of the current CSR agenda for addressing issues of governance. While extractive industries such as oil and gas generate relatively few jobs and local economic linkages compared with manufacturing or services industries, they have been blamed for distorting national economies and undermining good governance. Many oil-producing countries have suffered from the phenomenon known as the 'resource curse'. Despite being well endowed with natural resources, oil-producing countries have experienced economic underdevelopment, political mismanagement and military conflict, a finding supported by many quantitative and qualitative studies and accepted by World Bank and IMF economists (Gelb 1988; Ross 1999; Sachs and Warner 1999, 2001).

There are three principal negative societal effects of natural resource exports, which have been called the 'resource curse':

- *Impact on the economy*. Large foreign exchange inflows generated by extractive industries exports lead to the appreciation of a country's currency exchange rates, which makes it more difficult to export agricultural and manufacturing goods – a phenomenon known as Dutch disease. Extractive industries also draw capital, labour and entrepreneurial activity away from non-resource sectors such as manufacturing and agriculture, thereby stifling the development of those sectors. Not surprisingly, it has been shown that resource-rich countries have had lower economic growth rates than countries without these resources over the long term (Corden 1984; Sachs and Warner 1999, 2001).

- *Impact on governance.* Extractive industries exports may undermine good governance and political accountability to society. Given their dependence on extractive industries revenue, governments in resource-rich countries may neglect non-resource taxation and may have fewer incentives to nurture other economic sectors and improve the quality of institutions. It has been shown that resource-rich countries have higher levels of corruption and lower levels of education than non-resource rich countries (Gylfason 2001; Leite and Weidmann 1999).

- *Impact on conflict.* The extraction of natural resources requires little human co-operation and tends to be less affected by violent conflicts than manufacturing or service industries. Because multinational companies can build the necessary infrastructure, including access roads, they are able to provide their own security and – being enclave economies – they rely little on local business linkages. Thus, governments in resource-rich countries have less incentive to ensure economic and political stability. In addition, the prospect of gaining control over natural resource revenues may encourage the formation of rebel groups and separatist movements. It has been shown that a country's dependence on natural resources dramatically increases the threat of armed conflict (Collier and Hoeffler 1998, 2000; Elbadawi and Sambanis 2000; Keen 1998).

As one expert summarised the fate of oil-exporting countries: '[T]heir reality is sobering: countries that depend on oil for their livelihood are among the most economically troubled, the most authoritarian, and the most conflict-ridden in the world' (Karl 2005, 21).

Both developing countries such as Nigeria and Venezuela and developed countries such as the United Kingdom and the Netherlands have suffered from the resource curse; indeed, the term 'Dutch disease' (relating to the appreciation of a country's currency exchange rates) originally referred to the economic problems caused by natural gas exports in the Netherlands. The potential effects of the resource curse were greatest in countries with high dependence on oil and gas revenues, such as Algeria and Nigeria (see Table 6.1).

In most developed economies, the effects of the resource curse were minimised thanks to the diversification of the economy and prudent government policy. Furthermore, a small number of resource-rich developing countries – in particular Botswana, Chile and Malaysia – have not only been able to beat the resource curse but have achieved high economic growth (Hojman 2002; Sarraf and Jiwanji 2001; Usui 1996). The biggest difference between successful and unsuccessful resource-rich countries was the quality of governance. In successful resource-rich countries, revenues from extractive industries exports were utilised to stimulate economic growth elsewhere in the economy, while the economy was insulated from resource-curse effects through government policies such as the establishment of 'revenue stabilisation' or a 'savings fund' (Stevens 2005). The differences between successful and less successful countries in terms of the local economic impact of the oil and gas sector are enormous. In Brazil and Malaysia, about 70 per cent of the goods and services purchased by oil companies is sourced locally; in Indonesia and Nigeria, the share of local content is only 25 per cent and 5 per cent, respectively (United Nations Conference on Trade and Development 2007, 141).

Given that skilful government policies and appropriate societal institutions can reduce or avoid the effects of the resource curse, the key challenge for resource-rich countries is how to improve macro-economic and macro-political conditions. In other words, the challenge is how to improve wider societal governance, which is defined here as 'the various ways through which social life is

TABLE 6.1: *Countries with highest dependence on oil and gas exports (percentage of total exports, five-year average), 2000–4*

Country	Percentage of total exports	Product description
Algeria	97.8	Oil and gas
Nigeria	97.8	Oil
Libya	96.9	Oil
Yemen	93.3	Oil and gas
Kuwait	92.9	Oil
Angola	92.2	Oil
Qatar	89.1	Oil, petrochemicals
Saudi Arabia	88.9	Oil
Brunei	88.3	Oil
Azerbaijan	86.6	Oil
Iran	86.3	Oil and gas
Venezuela	83.4	Oil
Turkmenistan	81.0	Gas
Oman	80.6	Oil
Gabon	79.5	Oil
Sudan	74.2	Oil
Syria	72.8	Oil
Bahrain	70.5	Oil
Trinidad and Tobago	61.3	Oil and gas
Kazakhstan	56.1	Oil and gas

Source: United Nations Conference on Trade and Development 2007, 87.

coordinated' (Heywood 2002, 6). A recent UN study on extractive industries pointed to the 'urgent need' to address societal governance:

Without a well-developed governance framework, there is an increased risk that benefits from extraction will not materialize, that fiscal systems will lead to uneven sharing of revenues, that lack of a coherent and concerted development strategy will lead to their misuse, that local populations will be left disappointed, and that environmental damage, health risk and conflicts will occur. (United Nations Conference on Trade and Development 2007, 96)

Recent research suggests that even the most enlightened and far-reaching CSR initiatives may face systemic constraints arising from the existing systems of societal governance. In their research on BP's wide-ranging initiatives to contribute to development in Azerbaijan, Gulbrandsen and Moe (2007) suggest that a shift of focus from micro-level CSR activities towards macro-level governance issues is crucial in addressing development issues. Similarly, in her work on CSR initiatives in the coffee sector, MacDonald (2007, 793) found that the focus of CSR initiatives on the industry's supply chains alone 'has limited their ability to advance those dimensions of worker and producer wellbeing that are shaped by a range of state and non-state actors' outside the supply chains. A number of other authors have recently pointed to the importance of linking CSR to wider societal governance (Blowfield and Frynas 2005; Frynas 2008; Tallontire 2007).

Tackling the governance challenge

Oil companies have, until recently, rejected the notion that they should actively address macro-level governance issues. Governance in a society is ultimately related to the role of the government, and companies have been reluctant to become drawn into the sphere of politics. As one example, a senior USAID official recounted in a private conversation how American corporations have been keen on getting involved in various development initiatives in education and health, but 'for instance, we couldn't get companies involved in party-building activities in Zambia.' In the words of one oil company manager interviewed: 'we cannot be government'.

While the notion of non-involvement in government affairs has not radically changed, a number of multinational oil companies including Shell, BP and Statoil now recognise that they can play a positive role in strengthening governance. BP in Azerbaijan is arguably by far the most wide-ranging attempt by a single company to address governance shortcomings. The company has publicly stated that it is prepared to 'engage in policymaking processes and offer assistance, as appropriate, on the development and implementation of policy agendas, which include for consideration addressing poverty alleviation, revenue management, and domestic energy' (quoted in Gulbrandsen and Moe 2007, 819). BP has co-operated with the government of Azerbaijan to facilitate expert advice on the management of the country's state oil fund and oil revenues. Furthermore, the company operates a regional development initiative to initiate large-scale and cross-regional development interventions in Georgia, Turkey and Azerbaijan, with the European Bank for Reconstruction and Development and the World Bank as partners. Governance is to be improved through 'civil society capacity building, strengthening the rule of law, and proffering expert advice and assistance' (Gulbrandsen and Moe 2007).

The initiatives by BP in Azerbaijan are exceptional in a number of ways, but other multinational companies also profess to contribute to better governance. Out of twenty oil and gas companies analysed for this chapter, eleven explicitly state that they address governance issues. However, the scope of governance initiatives is very narrow. All of the eleven companies have largely focused on a single governance issue: revenue transparency, which refers to openness and access to information with regard to company payments and government revenues from oil, gas and mining. Nine of these companies are based in developed countries. Only two out of eleven companies – Brazil's Petrobras and South Africa's Sasol – are based in emerging markets, which reflects the relative sophistication of these two companies in addressing CSR challenges (see Table 6.2).

TABLE 6.2: *Support for revenue transparency by selected oil companies in 2006*

Company	Country	Support for revenue transparency	Formal EITI supporter
BP	UK	+	+
Shell	UK	+	+
Chevron	USA	+	+
Exxon	USA	+	+
Statoil	Norway	+	+
Norsk Hydro	Norway	+	+
Total	France	+	+
ENI	Italy	+	+
Repsol	Spain	+	+
OMV	Austria		
CNOOC	China		
Sinopec	China		
Lukoil	Russia		
Gazprom	Russia		
MOL	Hungary		
Petrobras	Brazil	+	+
Petronas	Malaysia		
PKN Orlen	Poland		
PTT	Thailand		
Sasol	South Africa	+	

Revenue transparency is now regarded as the priority initiative to address governance in resource-rich countries by policy makers, the major oil companies and non-governmental organisations. It is assumed that transparency can contribute towards minimising the effects of the resource curse through beneficial political, economic and social effects (see next section). The main expected benefit of transparency is the reduction of corruption. Indeed, one expert on transparency stated: 'The word "transparency" is often used as a synonym for the absence of corruption. Transparency is also thought of as a solution or vaccine against corruption' (Henriques 2007, 137).

BP was a pioneering oil company in terms of revenue transparency. In 2001, BP announced that it would publish the following information annually on their operations in Angola: total net production by oil block; aggregate payments by the company to the state oil corporation Sonangol in respect of production-sharing contracts; and total taxes and levies paid by BP to the Angolan Government as a result of their operations. In the same year, BP disclosed some payments that the company made to the government of Azerbaijan. In a further unprecedented move, the company published various documents – including production-sharing agreements signed with the government of Azerbaijan – on a website in 2002. BP's actions on transparency were hailed as a major step by some non-governmental organisations, most notably Global Witness, a London-based NGO which has campaigned for the disclosure of such information by oil companies.

However, none of the other major oil companies followed BP's lead in offering to publish their payments to governments. According to interviews, the Angolan Government was highly displeased by BP's unilateral decision to publish payments to the government, and Angolan Government officials even threatened to expel BP from the country as a consequence. BP's experience in Angola demonstrated the collective action problem with regard to governance initiatives: most companies would benefit from improved governance in host countries, but companies may be reluctant to pursue governance initiatives because they may potentially suffer individually as a result.

BP's lesson in Angola partly informed the birth of the Extractive Industry's Transparency Initiative (EITI) (see Box 6.1). The EITI was launched in 2003 to improve the transparency of revenues paid by oil,

---

Box 6.1: Extractive Industry's Transparency Initiative

The Extractive Industry's Transparency Initiative (EITI) was launched at the suggestion of the UK Government in June 2003. The EITI describes itself as 'a coalition of governments, companies, civil society groups, investors and international organizations'. It aims to 'improve governance in resource-rich countries through the full publication and verification of company payments and government revenues from oil, gas and mining'.

Each EITI-implementing country commits itself to six EITI 'criteria':

1. Regular publication of all payments received by the government from oil, gas and mining companies.
2. Independent audits for all such payments, applying international auditing standards.
3. Checking of all payments by an independent administrator.
4. Inclusion of all oil, gas and mining companies, including state-owned enterprises.
5. Involvement of civil society in the design, monitoring and evaluation of the reporting process.
6. A work plan for the government, 'including measurable targets, a timetable for implementation and an assessment of potential capacity constraints'.

As of July 2008, twenty-three developing countries were EITI-implementing countries. They were: Azerbaijan, Cameroon, Congo, Democratic Republic of the Congo, East Timor, Equatorial Guinea, Gabon, Ghana, Guinea, Ivory Coast, Kazakhstan, Kyrgyzstan, Liberia, Madagascar, Mali, Mauritania, Mongolia, Niger, Nigeria, Peru, São Tomé and Príncipe, Sierra Leone and Yemen.

As of July 2008, the EITI was formally supported by sixteen oil and gas companies, including BG group (UK), BP (UK), Chevron (USA), ConocoPhilips (USA), Eni (Italy), Exxon (USA), Hess Corporation (USA), Marathon (USA), Pemex (Mexico), Petrobras (Brazil), Repsol YPF (Spain), Shell (UK/Netherlands), StatoilHydro (Norway), Talisman Energy (Canada), Total (France) and Woodside (Australia).

Source: EITI website at www.eitransparency.org/
(accessed 18 July 2008).

gas and mining companies to host governments, which in turn would limit corruption related to such revenues. A key strength of the initiative was that it would involve all companies in a member country, which avoids the collective action problems that BP faced in Angola. Another strength was the requirement to involve civil society and independent auditors, which helps to properly oversee the implementation of the EITI in a given country.

The establishment of a 'revenue savings fund' is one example of how revenue transparency can help towards reducing resource-curse effects. For instance, the creation of the State Oil Fund of the Azerbaijan Republic (SOFAZ) has to some extent protected the local economy in Azerbaijan from extreme currency appreciation and oil price fluctuations, by depositing a part of the country's oil revenues in an overseas account. SOFAZ became (in the words of the Economist Intelligence Unit) 'the most transparent government body in Azerbaijan (Economist Intelligence Unit 2006, 26). The establishment of SOFAZ was conducive to EITI membership, and the EITI helps to ensure the publication of annual data on Azerbaijani revenue flows. Beating the resource curse requires more than just a transparent revenue savings fund, but Azerbaijan achieved more in this respect than the majority of other resource-rich countries in the past.

The most far-reaching external policy initiative to avoid the pitfalls of the resource curse in an oil-producing country was the Revenue Management Program in Chad. The programme was initiated by the World Bank, and oil companies were not directly involved. The Chadian experiment yielded some positive societal benefits, and it helped to insulate the country from the resource curse for a number of years (see Box 6.2).

Potential and limitations of transparency

Transparency can contribute towards minimising the effects of the resource curse, but transparency initiatives are relatively young, and

---

Box 6.2: Revenue Management Program in Chad

In 1998, the World Bank and the government of Chad agreed on a revenue management programme, which was designed to ensure that future oil revenues would be used to the benefit of wider society. Ten per cent of Chad's direct oil revenues (dividends and royalties – as opposed to petroleum taxes) were to be placed in a London-based Future Generations Fund. Of the remainder, 80 per cent of royalties and 85 per cent of dividends were to be devoted to priority sectors including education, health and social services, rural development and infrastructure. Revenues were transferred into an escrow account in London.

The Revenue Management Program established mechanisms for overseeing the use of oil revenues. This included an oversight committee with participants from politics, the judiciary and civil society. The World Bank also strengthened public sector capacity, including providing Chad's ministry of finance with training in public resources management.

Between the start of oil production in July 2003 and June 2006, the country had earned US$537 million in direct oil revenues, of which US$295 million was reportedly allocated to 'priority sectors' including health, education and roads. The Revenue Management Program also helped to avoid a number of resource-curse effects, including the appreciation of the country's exchange rate. The country's real exchange rate increased by only 2 per cent over the period 2004–5 – at a time when oil export growth was highest.

However, the government of Chad unilaterally reneged on earlier agreements on priority spending and abolished the Future Generations Fund in December 2005. The World Bank consequently temporarily suspended all loans to Chad in January 2006. A new agreement between the World Bank and Chad was signed in July 2006, which provided the government of Chad with greater autonomy in the spending of oil revenues. Finally, the World Bank withdrew from the Revenue Management Program in September 2008.

Sources: World Bank website at www.worldbank.org/
(accessed 2 April 2008); Gould and Winters 2007; Kojucharov 2007.

---

few academic studies have been carried out to date on the most appropriate use of transparency initiatives and the actual impact of transparency. However, extensive quantitative studies clearly demonstrate the positive development effects of transparency (Alt and Lassen 2006a,b; Gelos and Wei 2005; Shi and Svensson 2002).

Benefits of transparency initiatives

There is strong evidence that transparency has positive political, economic and social effects:

- **Political effects.** Transparency improves informational flows between the rulers and the ruled. It ensures that financial flows are reported to a wide audience in a publicly accessible, comprehensive and easily understandable manner. Studies show that transparency in revenue and expenditure flows reduces the scope for corruption and generating political budget cycles, which means that politicians have less scope to overspend budgets at certain times (e.g., during election years) (Alt and Lassen 2006a,b). In turn, informational flows improve the management of these revenues, for example by the creation of effective 'revenue savings funds' mentioned earlier. Political leaders also benefit in that their policies and statements gain higher credibility, the reputation and legitimacy of the government and public institutions are strengthened and relationships with international organisations and aid donors are improved.
- **Economic effects.** Transparency improves a country's credibility among foreign investors and the international banking community. There is evidence that high-transparency countries enjoy lower costs of borrowing in sovereign debt markets, and investment funds make larger investments in high-transparency countries (Gelos and Wei 2005; Glennerster and Shin 2003). Adoption of transparency initiatives can therefore contribute to an improved investment climate by providing a clear signal to investors and the international financial institutions that the government is committed to improved accountability and good governance.
- **Social effects.** The positive political and economic effects of transparency can have many indirect social effects. By improving the quality of government policy, lowering the costs of government investment and attracting foreign capital, transparency indirectly results in various positive impacts, including contributing to

poverty reduction. Furthermore, a general climate of transparency empowers civil society groups to monitor budget decisions at the micro-level: for instance, the award of specific contracts in the health service (see Box 6.3). Central government transparency therefore has role-model effects for other parts of economic and public life (Shultz 2004).

Box 6.3: Transparency in health services

According to Transparency International (2006), more than US$3 trillion is spent world-wide on health services annually, but probably hundreds of billions are lost every year through corruption, overspending on medical supplies or bottlenecks in budget execution. In gold-exporting Ghana, it has been estimated that as much as half of the overall budget allocated to clinics and hospitals did not actually reach them, and 80 per cent of non-salary funds did not reach health facilities.

Transparency improves the effectiveness of health services and reduces health care costs. There is evidence that transparency has two main positive effects on health services:

- Central government transparency can encourage the development of formal transparency in the health sector, such as independent audits, release of information about tendering processes, dissemination of information about costs of procurement and transparency in overseas development aid. For example, a study from Argentina demonstrated that the variation across hospitals in prices of medical supplies was reduced by 50 per cent after the Argentinian Government began to disseminate information about how much hospitals were paying for supplies (Transparency International 2006).
- Transparency of government spending can encourage civil society groups to monitor budget decisions at the micro-level. In Mexico, FUNDAR – a centre for the analysis and research of budget issues – started a project to examine how state funds were spent to address maternal mortality. In an alliance with other civil society organisations, FUNDAR produced over 100 pages of data, analysis and argument and disseminated this analysis widely in Mexico. As a result of civil society efforts, the budget of an important maternal health programme increased almost tenfold (Shultz 2004).

There is thus abundant evidence that transparency potentially has many benefits for countries that adopt it. Indeed, high-transparency countries consistently perform better than low-transparency countries on different measures. One key positive impact, which has been studied in some detail, is lower debt accumulation. Statistical analysis by Alt and Lassen (2006a,b) clearly shows that high-transparency countries have consistently lower government budget deficits and consequently lower debt levels than low-transparency countries. Lower debt accumulation is crucial to poverty reduction, given that country indebtedness is in itself a cause of poverty. Twelve out of the world's twenty-five most resource-rich countries and six of the world's most oil-rich countries were classified by the World Bank as Highly Indebted Poor Countries, displaying some of the worst Human Development Indicators (World Bank 2003, 12).

However, most studies on transparency suggest that a number of conditions must be fulfilled in order to maximise the positive impact of transparency. Based on the literature, at least three conditions are necessary: (1) free media; (2) involvement of civil society; and (3) timing of introduction of transparency. In other words, the success of the EITI depends on these three conditions, which we shall discuss in the following section.

Conditions of success and limitations of transparency

As revealed by previous research, the success of transparency initiatives in the oil and gas sector depends on the following conditions:

- **Media**. Evidence suggests that independent media is an important tool for increasing accountability and the beneficial effects of transparency (Besley and Prat 2006). Better flows of information about revenues and spending allow the public and interest groups to observe the causes and effects of fiscal policy and thereby improve political accountability. There is anecdotal evidence, for example, that the publication of the federation account in Nigeria provided journalists with a powerful tool to scrutinise the expenditure of local government authorities and helped to increase accountability. The success of EITI depends on reporting revenue flows to a wide audience, and the media therefore assist the EITI process.

- **Civil society.** It has been found that the involvement of private associations and non-profit organisations is crucial for the success of any anti-corruption and transparency initiatives and can be even more important than the role of the media (Rose-Ackermann 1999, 167–71). Watchdog groups such as Transparency International or Kazakhstan Revenue Watch have a crucial role to play in monitoring and disseminating information, ensuring that larger development goals are pursued, influencing policy and training local civil society groups to understand the relevant issues. Civil society engagement can have tangible development outcomes. It has been reported that the budget allocation for public services (including anti-poverty programmes) in Indonesia's capital Jakarta increased from 30 per cent to 68 per cent in the period 2000–4, as a direct result of civil society budget advocacy initiatives (Shultz 2004).

- **Timing.** Experience suggests that once extractive export revenues start flowing, 'governments find it difficult to avoid a diversion from development projects to spending for political advantage' (Bell *et al.* 2004). Once the government begins to receive oil and gas revenues, third parties such as the World Bank and EITI lose much of their bargaining power in persuading host governments to adopt principles of good governance and transparency (Frynas and Paulo 2007; Gould and Winters 2007). Therefore, the potential development benefits of transparency can be maximised if transparency measures are adopted *before* the start of extractive operations. In Azerbaijan and in Chad (see above) the revenue management initiatives were established before the start of the actual oil boom, at a time when external actors had greater bargaining power.

Therefore, transparency initiatives are unlikely to be successful in autocratic regimes, which do not allow a free press and a free civil society. As one author wrote in summary, 'the success stories in resource revenue management have occurred where there is visionary political leadership that understands the need for explicit policies for economic management and accountability and where civil society and the media have the capacity to press for good governance of resource wealth' (Shankleman 2006).

One of the six EITI criteria stipulates that civil society organisations are involved from the outset. However, EITI cannot change the fact that most EITI-implementing countries, such as Azerbaijan or Equatorial Guinea, simply do not have free media or a free civil society.

Table 6.3 demonstrates that most oil-producing countries lack the necessary preconditions for the success of transparency. The table lists the thirty largest oil-producing nations in the world and indicates which countries have 'political and civil freedom' and 'media freedom', using the 2007 rankings by Freedom House – an international organisation that compiles 'freedom' rankings every year. Out of twenty-four oil-producing countries in the developing world, only five – Mexico, Brazil, Indonesia, India and Argentina – have political and civil freedom, while a number of other countries are classified as 'partly free'. Of these twenty-four countries, not a single one has a genuinely free press. Out of seven EITI participants listed in Table 6.3, not a single country has a genuinely free civil society or free press, while a few countries such as Nigeria are classified as 'partly free'.

The six largest oil-producing nations from the developed world – the United States, Canada, Norway, the United Kingdom, Australia and Denmark – have both a free civil society and a free press. Indeed, previous studies that found positive effects of transparency have often focused on developed countries (Alt and Lassen 2006a,b; Besley and Prat 2006). In contrast, all EITI participants are developing countries, and there is no research to demonstrate that the EITI actually helped

TABLE 6.3: *Civil liberties and media freedom in largest oil-producing countries in 2007*

Country	Oil production (thousand barrels per day)	EITI participant	Political and civil freedom	Media freedom
United States	6,895		+	+
Canada	3,041		+	+
Norway	2,968		+	+
United Kingdom	1,809		+	+
Australia	554		+	+
Denmark	377		+	+
Saudi Arabia	11,114			
Russia	9,552			
Iran	4,267			
Mexico	3,760		+	±
China	3,627			
Venezuela	2,937		±	
United Arab Emirates	2,751			
Kuwait	2,643		±	±
Nigeria	2,580	+	±	±
Algeria	2,016			
Iraq	1,833			
Libya	1,751			
Brazil	1,715		+	±
Kazakhstan	1,356	+		
Angola	1,233			
Indonesia	1,128		+	±
Qatar	1,045			

TABLE 6.3: *(cont.)*

Country	Oil production (thousand barrels per day)	EITI participant	Political and civil freedom	Media freedom
India	784		+	±
Oman	779			
Malaysia	767		±	
Argentina	725		+	±
Egypt	696			
Colombia	554		±	±
Ecuador	541		±	±
Syria	458			
Azerbaijan	452	+		
Yemen	426	+	±	
Vietnam	398			
Equatorial Guinea	356	+		
Sudan	355			
Thailand	265			±
Republic of the Congo	246	+		±
Gabon	234	+	±	
Brunei	206			

Notes: + free
± partly free
Sources: BP Statistical Review of World Energy 2007; Freedom House 'Freedom in the World 2007' and 'Freedom of the Press 2007' surveys at www.freedomhouse.org (accessed 20 March 2008).

to bring any positive political, economic and social benefits to member countries (see the following section).

By implication, the optimism over the adoption of transparency initiatives by developing countries is, at best, exaggerated and, at worst, misguided. The preconditions for the success of the EITI are simply not present in countries such as Azerbaijan and Equatorial Guinea. Indeed, more than five years since the launch of the EITI, not a single country has so far complied with the EITI validation; in the words of the EITI itself, 'no country has been formally validated against the EITI indicators' (EITI website at www.eitransparency.org/compliantcountries, accessed 31 March 2008).

The World Bank-led Revenue Management Program in Chad mentioned earlier ultimately failed. While the programme yielded some economic and social benefits, academic research has demonstrated that it fell far short of the expected outcomes (Gould and Winters 2007; Kojucharov 2007; Pegg 2006). From the start, it became clear that the programme had shortcomings, and the Chadian Government was able to divert some earmarked funds towards other purposes. In 2006, Chad's agreement with the World Bank was renegotiated and watered down, and the 'Future Generations Fund' was scrapped, as President Idriss Deby demanded more access to the country's oil revenues in order to purchase weapons for use against his enemies. There have been suggestions that the actions of oil companies further undermined the World Bank's efforts; after threats from the Chadian Government in 2006, the US company Chevron and the Malaysian company Petronas agreed to pay undisclosed sums to the government which escaped the Revenue Management Program. Finally, the World Bank withdrew from the Revenue Management Program in September 2008, stating that 'Regrettably, it became evident that the arrangements that had underpinned the Bank's involvement in the Chad/Cameroon pipeline project were not working' (World Bank 2008).

A frequently cited reason for the problems of the World Bank programme in Chad was timing. On the one hand, Chad's government had more bargaining power in 2006 than in 2003 thanks to the inflow of oil revenues; thus, it was in a position to renegotiate previous agreements. On the other hand, the World Bank failed to effectively create the mechanisms for overseeing the use of oil revenues (including a strong and well-resourced oversight committee) *before* the start of oil production in 2003. While World Bank officials emphasised the importance of 'sequencing' (which means encouraging capacity-building before allowing oil infrastructure construction), pipeline construction already started four months after project approval, and oil production started one year ahead of schedule. In effect, neither the project oversight committee nor Chad's government institutions were effectively prepared for the inflow of oil revenues, nor were the rules for handling oil revenues effectively established. One observer noted in 2007: 'Nearly seven years into the project and four years since the first batch of oil exports, Chad, the World Bank, and the oil consortium are still trying to negotiate the rules and mechanisms for calculating and distributing oil revenues' (quoted in Kojucharov 2007, 488).

In more general terms, the problem of timing implies that third parties such as the World Bank and the EITI have even less leverage in established oil-producing countries compared with Chad. In established oil-producing countries (particularly in those countries undergoing an oil boom), the government is less dependent on external aid and loans, it can obtain oil-backed loans from international banks and it can obtain unconditional loans and aid from new actors, including the government of China. In other words, the government can escape externally imposed conditions by the World Bank and other third parties. As the author of this book has previously argued, it is no coincidence that many oil-producing countries managed to defy the International Monetary Fund and the World Bank in different ways for a long time; for instance, the oil boom radically improved the bargaining power of Equatorial Guinea, and President Obiang was able to resist calls by the IMF for major macro-economic reforms as a result (Frynas 2004).

In addition to the three conditions of success identified above, the EITI initiative has inherent limitations, which we shall discuss in the next section.

Limitations of the EITI

Notwithstanding the existing conditions for success, the design and remit of the EITI also have inherent limitations. Above all, the EITI focuses on revenues, not spending.

Effective EITI implementation helps to reveal how much a government has earned from oil and gas, but this does not necessarily help to increase the accountability of government spending. For instance, while the Economist Intelligence Unit praised the accountability of SOFAZ (the revenue savings fund in Azerbaijan), it pointed out: 'International financial institutions have expressed concern that, although management of SOFAZ has proved relatively transparent, that accountability is lost once the funds are transferred for use into the state budget' (Economist Intelligence Unit 2006, 26). In the words of one recent study on Azerbaijan, 'The main weakness of EITI is the lack of reporting and monitoring of the government's spending of oil revenues' (Gulbrandsen and Moe 2007, 822).

Existing empirical evidence on the positive effects of transparency relates to how the money is spent, not how it is earned. All of the positive effects of transparency mentioned earlier – ranging from increased foreign investments to decreased corruption in the health service – relate to the scrutiny of government spending and *not* the scrutiny of government revenues.

Indeed, the premise of the EITI that revenue transparency provides benefits for implementing countries and investors is unproven and speculative, given that existing research focuses on government spending – not revenue transparency. Studies on transparency that found positive benefits of transparency focused on the transparency of spending and actual outcomes of spending. Previous research measured the transparency of individual countries according to quantitative indicators such as macro-economic forecasts (Gelos and Wei 2005), the publication of International Monetary Fund reports on the macro-economic performance of countries (Glennerster and Shin

2003) and the quality of government budget documentation (Alt and Lassen 2006a,b). All of these studies imply that the quality of decision-making on spending is crucial, in terms of complying with international norms and accounting standards, publication and independent verification of government budgets and the actual outcomes of decision-making. Not a single study quoted earlier focused specifically on the transparency of revenues; indeed, there appears to be an assumption among researchers that transparency of revenues is a secondary concern. In summary, there is no scientific basis for the assertion that revenue transparency leads to better social or economic outcomes.

Lessons from successful resource-rich countries further suggest that improving the quality of government spending provides the key to addressing governance challenges. It has been found that the economic success of resource-rich countries such as Botswana, Indonesia, Malaysia and Chile had a common characteristic: prudence in spending extractive revenues. A study by Paul Stevens graphically portrayed the approach of successful countries:

> When money was spent, it went on productive activities. Conspicuous consumption and gigantomania were constrained although not entirely absent. Much of the revenue trickled down to the private sector boosting savings and investment. (Stevens 2005)

Prudent spending was supported by government policies that helped to insulate countries from the negative effects of the resource curse such as revenue stabilisation funds, and policies that helped to stimulate the private sector in other parts of the economy. As a result, these countries have been able to grow other economic sectors, in particular, manufacturing. Statistics demonstrate that the per capita GDP growth in non-resource sectors was high in the four countries mentioned above (Stevens 2005).

The EITI initiative is unlikely to duplicate the success of Botswana or Chile because it does little or nothing to improve the quality of government spending. From this perspective, policy initiatives by the World Bank and the IMF have greater likelihood of success precisely because they deal with government spending. The World Bank initiative in Chad focused on spending, as mentioned earlier. Similarly, the IMF encourages the publication of country reports that deal with broader transparency and the quality of governance in government finances; these include Reports on the Observance of Standards and Codes (ROSCs) which summarise the respective countries' observance of standards and codes related to auditing, banking supervision, corporate governance, and monetary and financial policy transparency, among others. Indeed, one quantitative study on transparency specifically found that the publication of IMF reports such as ROSCs contributes towards better informed markets and lower costs of borrowing for governments in participating countries (Glennerster and Shin 2003). In contrast to the World Bank and the IMF, the EITI does not deal with issues of wider transparency and governance of public finances and is unlikely to yield similar positive results.

In addition to its narrow focus, one key dilemma of the EITI is that (in the words of one oil and gas sector insider) it 'shifted the responsibility back to government'. The EITI focuses on the co-operation between the UK Government and host governments in developing countries; the initiative does not assign an active role to oil, gas and mining companies in improving governance. The failure to assign a clearer role to companies constrains the pressure on host governments, because the UK Government or the World Bank sometimes have less influence over host governments than the multinational companies.

In summary, the main governance initiative in the oil and gas sector – the EITI – has serious shortcomings and is unlikely to duplicate the success stories of countries such as Botswana or Chile. It also fails to draw on the companies' resources in influencing governments, which we discuss in the next section.

Undermining governance through corporate activity

Most oil company executives tend to reject the notion that they could play a constructive role in helping to address governance issues, and they have a legitimate concern over corporate involvement in the political process. However, such a stance denies the reality that (1) multinational companies already intervene in the political process to attain corporate objectives (e.g., lobbying for new legislation) (Frynas et al. 2006; Shaffer and Hillman 2000); (2) corporate activities such as tax avoidance and lobbying may be contributing to governance failures (Henriques 2007; Utting 2007); and (3) under certain circumstances, multinational companies may benefit commercially from governance failures in developing countries (e.g., non-enforcement of certain government regulations or the ability of companies to negotiate more profitable agreements with governments) (Frynas 1998).

It has been suggested that the most effective business method for influencing political outcomes is collective action through organised interest groups. A vast literature demonstrates the impact of business interest groups on policy making (Mitnick 1993; Olson 1965; Schattschneider 1935). In addition, companies use many different methods of political influence, including political donations, PR and expert advice, which can yield them many business benefits including corporate influence over government policies, better information and reduced uncertainty (Getz 1993; Hillman and Hitt 1999; Keim and Zeithaml 1986).

Oil companies are members of interest groups including industry associations such as the American Petroleum Institute, single issue groups such as the Global Climate Coalition and cross-industry lobbying groups such as the European Round Table of Industrialists, which in turn influence government policies. In line with the influential theory of collective action (Olson 1965), oil companies are likely to have high political power because there is a relatively small number of big players in the industry that wield high economic power. Thus, the American Petroleum Institute is more influential than, for instance, a small business association. Large multinational oil companies are also powerful enough to single-handedly affect political outcomes in a country. At the extreme, a single company that has a dominant economic position in a country can be particularly influential, as exemplified by BP in Azerbaijan (see above). Companies often use that influence to attain corporate goals. Previous research by the author of this book points to the competitive advantages that oil companies can strategically draw from the political process (Frynas 1998; Frynas *et al.* 2006).

Firms are able to influence the institutions that affect them not only through involvement in the political process, but also by influencing technical standards, sources of funding or the media. For instance, in technical committees, subcommittees and working groups of the International Organization for Standardization (ISO), representatives of interest groups including firms and consumer bodies are treated as equal partners in shaping the agenda of the ISO. Among other things, multinational companies actively worked on developing the new ISO 26000 CSR standard. Indeed, an oil company manager from Exxon – W. James Bover – became chairman of ISO's technical committee on petroleum products and lubricants.[1] The example of the ISO may thus help to partly explain the corporate preference for voluntary agreements rather than formal government regulation, which allows firms to negotiate relatively favourable standards. In addition to the ISO, business lobby groups have played a formal role in a number of important international fora, which allowed them to gain influence over the political process related to social and environmental issues (see Table 6.4).

At this point, it should not be assumed that the use of influence by oil companies automatically has a negative impact. Indeed,

---

[1] For the list of technical committees, see the ISO website at www.iso.ch/meme/memento.html (accessed 12 November 2000 and 7 June 2006).

TABLE 6.4: *Level of formal access for business interest groups*

Level of access	Method of access	Example
High	Official function Advisory function	ISO standards US delegation in GATT
Moderate	Consultation Expression of opinion	Kyoto Protocol World Bank Extractive Industries Review
Low	No access	–

corporate political activities can encourage higher social, environmental and governance standards. For instance, it has been shown that lobbying by firms can help towards more stringent environmental regulations (McWilliams *et al.* 2002).

However, the actions of companies often have negative political consequences. It has been argued, for instance, that oil companies in Azerbaijan 'have (inadvertently at times) backed the Aliev government's intimidation of dissidents through outright bribery, patronizing only government-favoured media or businesses, and eschewing extended contacts with the political opposition' (Chen 2007, 43). A suggestion of a meeting with opposition politicians in Azerbaijan was met with 'less than no interest' by the oil companies (Gulbrandsen and Moe 2005, 59). One scholar noted that 'the warm and cozy relations of the Azerbaijani government with trans-national oil companies ensure the flow of funds at the expense of state and democracy building in the country' (Valiyev 2006, quoted in Chen 2007, 44).

In many oil-producing countries such as Libya and Venezuela, oil revenues have been shown to prolong authoritarian rule (Karl 1997; Vandewalle 1998). For instance, it is no coincidence that some of Africa's longest-serving heads of state come from oil-producing countries, including Bongo in Gabon (the country's president since 1967), dos Santos in Angola (1979), Obiang in Equatorial Guinea (1979) and Qadaffi in Libya (1969). Indeed, statistical analysis conducted by Michael Ross on 113 countries over the period 1971–97 provided evidence that oil and gas exports are strongly associated with authoritarian rule. In general terms, the study suggested that extractive exports concentrated in the hands of a relatively small number of actors have anti-democratic effects, while – for instance – more 'decentralised' agricultural exports have not. Michael Ross concluded that 'the oil-impedes-democracy claim is both valid and statistically robust' (Ross 2001, 356).

Corporate political activities may also have a negative impact through influencing social policy. As Peter Utting – Deputy Director of the UN Research Institute for Social Development – has pointed out, companies often use their political power to advance causes that have negative societal consequences, such as weakening of labour rights, tax avoidance or privatisation of basic services. Utting noted:

> Many of the world's largest corporations and business associations actively promote CSR while simultaneously lobbying forcefully for macroeconomic, labour market and other social policies associated with forms of labour market flexibilisation, deregulation, and fiscal 'reform' that can result in the weakening of institutions and systems of social protection.   (Utting 2007, 701)

Whether they are a force for good or bad, companies clearly use political influence, which in turn affects governance. Therefore, the controversy is not merely about the legitimacy of firms influencing government but rather about the actual manner of using political influence and about the transparency of firms regarding their political activities. Even if companies have done nothing wrong, by not disclosing their corporate lobbying activities they open themselves up to allegations that they may have something to hide about their political involvement or that they only intervene in the political process when it suits them.

A leading recent book on corporate transparency suggests that even the most transparent companies remain less than open about topics such as corruption and lobbying. The book notes: 'The extent of voluntary disclosure of lobbying activities by companies is very limited, to the extent that currently it is rare to find any voluntary reporting on lobbying expenditure or activities (Henriques 2007, 154).

Company reporting on corruption is also very limited, even by companies with highly developed codes of conduct. Henriques specifically points to the examples of Shell and BP. Shell, for instance, limits corruption reporting to the number of 'violations' explicitly reported to the audit committee of the board of Royal Dutch/Shell, and providing specific figures for Nigeria. However, as Henriques points out, the company fails to report on the nature of legal prosecutions, the use of agents or whistle-blowing – all of which are crucial to understanding both the problem of corruption and the company's ability to deal with the problem.

A 2008 report by Transparency International on the oil and gas sector supports the general findings by Henriques. The report analysed forty-two leading oil companies (both multinationals and domestic state-owned companies) in twenty-one countries of operation with regard to revenue transparency. The report suggested that the exclusive focus on the reporting of payments to governments is not sufficient to generating a climate of transparency. It stated:

> Revenue transparency by oil and gas companies is comprised of more than just reporting on payments to home governments on a country-by-country basis. It also requires disclosure of operations data and anti-corruption programmes both of which support such transparency and enable its sustainability by the company. (Transparency International 2008, 24)

The key finding of the Transparency International report was that the majority of the forty-two companies analysed 'do not make sufficient efforts to report on their payments to host governments on a country-by-country basis or to disclose the accompanying information on their operations and anti-corruption programmes' (Transparency International 2008, 24).

Therefore, while companies publicly support transparency, they appear only to select a few areas for openness, and they continue to be secretive about other areas. Indeed, CSR reporting and 'transparency initiatives' play a key role in influencing the media and public opinion because they help to portray firms as responsible citizens that care about people and the environment as much as about profits. As one study pointed out a long time ago, the influence of interest groups may indeed be greatest when 'disguised as altruistic, nonpartisan or patriotic interest' (Ray 1972), which can in turn help towards (to borrow from the vocabulary of Jürgen Habermas) 'procurement of legitimation'. Reporting on CSR lends itself perfectly to positively influencing external perceptions because it helps to disguise the real self-interest of firms. Henriques (2007, 150) commented that it is ironic that CSR or sustainability reports 'were originally conceived as mechanisms for companies to demonstrate that they were being influenced by their stakeholders, rather than vehicles for the opposite'.

In summary, companies use political influence to attain corporate goals related to profit maximisation, but they rarely use that influence to encourage improvements in governance. While CSR initiatives largely fail to encourage better governance, corporate activities may actually undermine governance.

Conclusion

Governance remains the main challenge for extractive industries. Yet this chapter has demonstrated that the current CSR agenda barely addresses governance issues. One exception is transparency, which has been supported by a number of multinational companies. Indeed, this chapter pointed to abundant evidence that transparency can yield many positive effects – ranging from increased foreign investment to decreased corruption in health services. However, the effectiveness of the current transparency initiatives – principally the EITI – is severely constrained. On the one hand, most oil-producing countries lack the conditions for the success of transparency initiatives. On the other hand, the EITI is constrained by its focus on revenue transparency – as opposed to transparency of government spending. Indeed, there is no scientific basis to support the premise of the EITI that revenue transparency leads to better social or economic outcomes.

In the face of the limitations of the EITI, the World Bank and the IMF may offer alternative mechanisms for improving governance in resource-rich countries. Indeed, in April 2008, the World Bank president, Robert Zoellick, announced a new initiative to help developing countries manage their natural resource revenues. The initiative, labelled 'The Extractive Industries Transparency Initiative Plus Plus' (EITI++), goes beyond the EITI by offering resource-rich countries World Bank assistance in designing contracts, monitoring operations, collecting taxes and, above all, spending the revenues effectively. The first two countries to implement the initiative are scheduled to be Guinea and Mauritania, two countries that have not yet experienced a natural resources boom. While details on the new initiative are still scarce at the time of writing, the World Bank initiative has certainly more merits than the current corporate and policy agenda on governance.

None the less, both the EITI and the new World Bank initiative fail to address the question of how multinational companies can be usefully integrated into improving governance. The author of this book believes that companies have a role to play in better governance in the countries where they operate. As this chapter has demonstrated, multinational companies are political actors already, and they use their influence to pursue corporate objectives. In many countries, ranging from Equatorial Guinea to Azerbaijan, Exxon or BP has more influence than the World Bank or other external actors. At the very least, multinational companies could use this influence to persuade governments to sign up to the EITI++ initiative, to publish Reports on the Observance of Standards and Codes (ROSCs) or to spend a greater portion of oil revenues on health and education. At the moment, companies continue to neglect the macro-level problems in their industry and the related governance issues.

Most multinational companies do not even accept that they have a responsibility for macro-level issues – issues concerning the society-wide impact of the oil and gas industry. Indeed, a Norwegian study of four multinational oil companies – Exxon, Shell, BP and Total – demonstrated that company executives do not fully acknowledge the resource-curse phenomenon. All companies continue to claim that they mainly benefit the countries in which they operate, despite the overwhelming evidence of the resource curse. In the words of the Norwegian researchers, 'this means that they [oil companies] do not fully consider the company's impact on the public in host countries' (Skjærseth et al. 2004).

The contention is not that a single company should accept the responsibility for the adverse impact of the entire oil and gas sector on the host country. Rather, the unwillingness of both companies and governments to face up to the reality of the resource curse constrains the CSR agenda. In simple terms: if one does not acknowledge the source of a problem, it may be difficult to consider the most appropriate solutions for it.

In conclusion, CSR debates appear to have marginalised debates on governance and macro-level solutions to complex society-wide problems. There is a real danger that a narrow focus on CSR, local community projects or the EITI may divert attention from broader political, economic and social solutions for such problems.

SEVEN

Conclusions and recommendations

This book set out to understand Corporate Social Responsibility (CSR) and particularly its potential and limitations for addressing key 'challenges' in the business–society relationship: the environment, development and governance. The oil and gas industry served as a window to a better understanding of what CSR can or cannot accomplish. This chapter briefly summarises the book's findings and provides recommendations for companies and policy makers.

Potential and limitations of CSR

The evidence in this book suggests that CSR has the greatest potential for addressing environmental challenges. Corporate reporting on the environment is steadily improving, new environmentally friendly technologies are being developed and tangible improvements are being made by some companies. Environmental challenges benefit from the specific expertise that companies possess, as technical and managerial skills greatly assist environmental improvements. Most crucially, environmental initiatives appear to lead to win-win outcomes: the environmental impact of companies is reduced, while companies benefit from lower operating costs, better equipment and innovation.

In contrast, the evidence in this book suggests that CSR has less potential for addressing problems related to community development and governance. Companies could greatly benefit from better community relations and improved governance: fewer operational losses as a result of community dissatisfaction, less corruption, improved corporate reputations and so on. The host countries could also greatly benefit from improvements in human development and governance, in terms of increased private investment, higher levels of education, better public services and so on. However, companies appear to be reluctant to address issues of governance, while their approaches to community development are often ineffective.

This book suggests that there are two deeper underlying reasons why multinational companies fail to effectively address development and governance concerns. First, the 'business case for CSR' (that is, the use of social initiatives for attaining corporate objectives) sets limits on what such initiatives can achieve for broader society. While the business case has potential for successfully addressing environmental issues, making a business case for tackling poverty or governance failures is often much more difficult. Unlike development agencies, companies do not tend to prioritise overall development goals such as poverty reduction. Indeed, profit-maximising motives are often incompatible with good development practice; Chapter 5 demonstrates how corporate motives can be at odds with the development needs of local communities.

Second, multinational companies often fail to acknowledge the full extent of their interactions with society and politics, and they do not accept responsibility for macro-level issues – issues concerning the society-wide impact of their industry. While companies clearly exercise political influence, they tend to reject the notion that they could play a constructive role in helping to address governance failures. In general, CSR debates appear to have marginalised debates on governance and macro-level solutions to complex society-wide problems. Yet CSR initiatives will not be able to tackle some of the key social and environmental challenges without addressing governance.

Conversely, there are limitations to the extent to which companies can help towards improvements in governance. At the one extreme, a single company that has a dominant economic position in a country can be particularly influential when the government is willing to tolerate corporate assistance. Most notably, we briefly described in Chapter 6 how BP was able to influence public policy in Azerbaijan by providing expert advice to the government. At the other extreme, a single company can be powerless when faced with government power. Most notably, the governments of Venezuela and Russia have in recent years curtailed the commercial operations of the biggest foreign oil companies, effectively expropriating some of the assets of Shell, BP and Exxon. The governments of countries such as Venezuela and Russia appear to be hostile to the very presence of foreign oil companies (Cresswell 2008; Reed 2007). The remarkable contrast between Azerbaijan, on the one hand, and Venezuela and Russia, on the other, once again underlines the importance of context for the success of CSR initiatives.

Importance of context

This book focuses on the oil and gas sector and some of the lessons are specific to that sector. Above all, Chapter 6 shows that resource extraction creates particular economic, political and social problems. Many other economic sectors do not create such negative effects. Therefore, issues such as wider societal governance and revenue transparency may be less relevant to companies from other sectors. The nature of an industry determines CSR concerns, and any CSR guidelines, standards and assessments should be made with reference to the industry context.

By implication, the current focus on the establishment of universal CSR standards is problematic. Some universal standards such as the UN Global Compact may be too superficial for effective implementation. Other universal standards such as the reporting guidelines of the Global Reporting Initiative may be less appropriate than sector-specific standards such as the 2005 Oil and Gas Industry Guidance on Voluntary Sustainability Reporting (see Chapter 4).

The wider societal context is also crucial. The discussion of transparency in Chapter 6 demonstrated that civil society, media freedom and timing are some of the necessary conditions of success for voluntary initiatives. The same initiative that was successful in Brazil or South Africa may not work in China or Azerbaijan because some of the conditions of success are absent. It has been previously shown, for instance, that independent monitoring of working conditions in China may be difficult or even dangerous (Chan 2005), while defective timing and sequencing was largely responsible for the limited success of the World Bank-led governance initiative in Chad (Gould and Winters 2007). Indeed, the uneven spread of the conditions of success across the world explains the uneven development of CSR in different parts of the world. Evidence in this book suggests that Brazil's Petrobras and South Africa's Sasol have much more sophisticated CSR policies than oil companies from other emerging markets such as China and Russia; indeed, CSR is generally more developed in Brazil and South Africa than in China and Russia.

Therefore, the universal assumptions about the social and political conditions of success for CSR initiatives are unrealistic. As the author of this book has previously argued, 'Current CSR models assume responsive business interested in CSR, an active civil society willing to partner with business and a strong state able to provide an enabling environment for CSR, yet these conditions are absent in the majority of the world' (Newell and Frynas 2007). A crucial challenge for the CSR agenda is to explore the potential and limitations of CSR in contexts which lack certain conditions of success. A related challenge is either to compensate for the lack of conditions for success in some countries (for instance, using alternative channels of communications in countries without free media or a civil society) or to help improve those conditions by contributing to better societal governance.

Finally, and perhaps most importantly, the needs and expectations of stakeholders vary between different places. As we pointed out earlier, South Africans expect companies to tackle black empowerment and HIV/Aids (Hamann *et al.* 2005), Argentinians expect companies to tackle the social needs created by the 2001 economic crisis (Newell and Muro 2006), while Nigerians expect oil companies to provide basic infrastructure (Frynas 2001). The universal CSR standards may do little to help companies 'to do the right thing' in those specific contexts.

Importance of government

This book has repeatedly shown that a country's government is not merely an important element of the national context, within which companies operate. The actions or inaction of the government largely define the rights and responsibilities of companies. Indeed, the distinction between 'regulatory compliance' (companies complying with the law) and 'voluntary action beyond compliance' (CSR) depends crucially on the government.

The need for CSR is greatest in societies where the government has not been successful in providing public goods and effective regulation. At least in the short term, stakeholders may expect companies to fill in for government shortcomings, and voluntary action by companies may provide one of the few available channels for environmental remedy, better working conditions or health provision. However, effective CSR in these societies can be constrained by the lack of government support, corruption or lack of a civil society.

In societies where the government has been relatively successful in providing public goods and effective regulation, the expectations placed on companies are considerably lower but government action is still crucial. Chapter 4 shows that government action is still very important in situations when there is great potential for CSR to create 'win-win' outcomes, namely environmental protection. Even

CSR leaders require government pressure to motivate them to innovate, as the example of BP's carbon trading scheme demonstrated. Government pressure is even more important for companies that are slow in improving their environmental performance, which is to say the majority of companies. The reality is that some companies are much more active in environmental improvements than others because companies react differently to the economic opportunities for voluntary action. Companies have considerable technical and managerial expertise, and they have considerable potential for creativity, but they may be slow in recognising the economic opportunities from CSR, they may be risk-averse, they may find it difficult to re-engineer their internal management systems or they may sacrifice future economic opportunities for the sake of short-term considerations. Government pressure can help to reduce uncertainties about the future, improve the economic incentives for companies to act responsibly and ensure a level playing field for everyone.

There will be further pressures on governments and intergovernmental organisations to go beyond 'voluntary CSR' towards a formal legal framework for holding companies accountable for their actions. For instance, since the appointment of Professor John Ruggie as a special representative to the secretary-general of the United Nations in 2005, Ruggie's yearly reports to the UN have promoted a universal international legal framework for the liability of companies for human rights infringements. Ruggie's 2007 report to the UN Human Rights Council was unequivocal in advocating a significant role for formal regulation: 'History demonstrates that without adequate institutional underpinnings markets will fail to deliver their full benefits and may even become socially unsustainable' (Ruggie 2007, 3).

However, it is obvious that government regulation is not a panacea. Indeed, appeals by non-governmental organisations for more international regulation seem to ignore the many historical failures of formal regulatory approaches to social and environmental issues, especially in developing countries. At the same time, the world's social and environmental challenges cannot be successfully tackled without government. It follows that we need to learn more about the optimal balance of voluntary and mandatory, national and international, prescriptive and enabling regulation. Debates on CSR must move beyond unproductive calls *for* or *against* regulation towards studying new forms of 'shared' governance.

Recommendations for the business community

The limitations of CSR do not imply that private enterprises should do nothing about societal issues. Firms are pressured to engage with the social and environmental aspects of their operations, and they may benefit from the business opportunities that CSR offers.

Given the importance of the industry context, industry associations have an important role to play in spreading social and environmental practices. Companies would benefit from having a strong CSR champion at the industry level. Industry associations can claim to represent the collective interests of their members, they often have greater power than individual members and they have the resources to undertake strategic sector-wide initiatives. They can provide training and information on the benefits of CSR to their members, they can formalise the exchange of best practices, they can introduce common industry standards for social reporting or environmental practices, they can devise sector-wide guidelines on human rights, they can launch initiatives on governance and so on. The International Council on Mining and Metals (ICMM) could serve as a possible role model (see Box 7.1). Most industries, including the oil and gas sector, do not have a comparable organisation to represent them.

Individual companies can still do a lot to improve their relationship with wider society, and some of the key advice seems to be so simple that it almost does not warrant a repetition here. One of the

---

Box 7.1: International Council on Mining and Metals (ICMM)

The International Council on Mining and Metals (ICMM) was founded in 2001 with the vision of a 'viable mining, minerals and metals industry that is widely recognized as essential for modern living and a key contributor to sustainable development'. Its members include three of the world's biggest mining companies: BHP Billiton (Australia), Rio Tinto (UK) and Anglo American (UK). As of April 2008, ICMM consisted of sixteen companies and twenty-eight national mining and global commodities associations.

All member companies are required to implement the ICMM Sustainable Development Framework, which includes ten general principles, reporting guidelines (including sector-specific indicators developed in collaboration with the Global Reporting Initiative) and an independent assurance procedure (to evaluate the companies' compliance with the ten principles and reporting guidelines).

ICMM is also a formal supporter of the EITI on behalf of its member companies, in contrast to the oil and gas sector, where oil companies such as BP and Petrobras have individually supported the EITI.

Source: ICMM website at www.icmm.com (accessed 21 April 2008).

---

main limitations of CSR is that micro-level projects often do not amount to a greater whole. Without co-ordination with other companies and stakeholders, the impact of a CSR initiative may be limited, a project may not be located where it is most needed or efforts may be duplicated. Partnerships with governments, international organisations, non-governmental organisations and other companies can greatly help towards maximising the potential of CSR. The involvement of industry and other business associations may further maximise this potential. If CSR is really going to fulfil its societal promise, the business community needs to make a shift from micro-level projects to macro-level solutions.

Chapter 5 suggested that many voluntary initiatives fail to generate societal benefits because companies do not listen to their stakeholders properly. Stakeholder engagement is often superficial and brief, companies may listen to those stakeholders with the biggest bargaining power rather than to those whose interests are most affected or managers may simply make decisions based on the company's priorities without due regard for the interests of stakeholders. As we identified in Chapter 5, a crucial problem is that decisions on social and environmental initiatives are usually made in order to pursue corporate rather than stakeholder priorities, which in turn may limit the ability of CSR to bring significant benefits to stakeholders. It follows that companies sometimes need to step outside the 'business case' and think like stakeholders, so that the priorities of stakeholders do not become subordinate to corporate priorities. One author has argued that managers should accept that respect for social issues 'will sometimes require companies to make less than the maximum possible profits' (Parkinson 1999, 62). Somewhat paradoxically, in order to have greater corporate benefits from CSR and stakeholder engagement in the long-term, corporate leaders may have to convert to the view that stakeholder concerns are sometimes more important than profits.

Beyond Corporate Social Responsibility

Several possible scenarios for the future of CSR beyond the year 2015 have been predicted (Ward and Smith 2006; White 2005). At one extreme, CSR may decline as a result of a severe long lasting global recession or another serious adverse event. At the other extreme, CSR may help towards systematically changing many business practices. The reality will probably lie somewhere between these two extremes. From a long-term perspective, however, the CSR concept may yet turn out to be short-lived and it may be replaced by 'corporate citizenship', 'accountability' or something entirely new. Indeed, we need to go beyond the CSR concept in order to maximise the positive contributions that business can make to society.

Experience to date suggests that CSR tools usually fail to transform the day-to-day running of the whole organisation. Even among the most socially responsible companies investigated in this book, CSR initiatives are often conducted in parallel to 'business-as-usual' activities, which may destroy many of the positive gains of these initiatives. The payment of taxes to unaccountable governments, private investment in countries with bad human rights records, relocation of jobs from one country to another, corporate lobbying of governments or tax avoidance may have negative consequences for society. Many taken-for-granted business practices are simply at odds with good corporate citizenship. Even if no harm is done, companies themselves realise that their main contribution to society is through paying taxes to governments, providing jobs and investment or – in the case of the energy sector – supplying energy. The key issues in the business–society relationship are economic and political, yet these issues tend to be ignored in CSR debates, and they tend to be excluded from the contents of CSR standards.

This book implies that the current focus of the CSR agenda on strictly 'social' and 'environmental' issues is problematic. With reference to the oil and gas sector, Chapter 6 suggested that the economic impact of private investment can be much more damaging than the 'social' or 'environmental' impact. Indeed, senior company executives understand the importance of addressing economic and political issues. A 2007 survey by the consultancy firm McKinsey among 2,687 senior executives from around the world asked the question 'Which three issues are likely to have the most impact, positive or negative, on shareholder value for companies in your industry over the next five years?' The response that recurred most often was environmental issues (48 per cent of executives), which is largely due to the recent concern with climate change. The other responses included: 'political influence and political involvement of companies' (25 per cent of executives), 'health care benefits and other employee benefits' (24 per cent), 'job losses and offshoring' (24 per cent), 'privacy, data security' (22 per cent), 'pension, retirement benefits' (22 per cent) (McKinsey & Company 2007). A number of these issues – including the political involvement of firms and job losses – are not even mentioned in current CSR discussions. Indeed, it is doubtful that voluntary CSR approaches are capable of tackling these issues.

While I do not propose a radical new approach to business–society relations, it may be useful to finish this book by briefly exploring ideas for alternative approaches to addressing the societal impact of business.

Given the importance of economics in shaping business practices, one needs to look much more closely at the rules governing the market, including terms of international trade, market structure and rules for foreign investment. Instead of relying on voluntary corporate initiatives, the responsibilities of business could conceivably be incorporated into the rules governing the market, such as, for instance, those governing regional economic trade agreements, international treaties or bilateral investment treaties between countries. There are already a few examples of rewriting international rules; for instance, the European Union has various rules protecting its citizens from irresponsible corporate behaviour and a bilateral agreement between the governments of the United States and Chile has a chapter on 'corporate stewardship'.

Encouraging more responsible business also requires new models of corporate governance. Recent evidence suggests that voluntary corporate initiatives cannot succeed in advancing societal goals without changes in corporate governance regimes, such as, for instance, the mandatory inclusion of employee representatives on the boards of trustees of pension funds, mandatory disclosure practices or government-enforced freedom of association (Bonvin 2007; Deakin and Hobbs 2007; Jones et al. 2007). Policy makers should make a concerted effort to rewrite company law and other regulatory instruments to increase the power of 'non-traditional stakeholders' and to require companies to become more transparent about all of their activities. Corporate governance reforms will help companies to make better social and environmental choices and to justify these choices in front of shareholders. Policy makers – including national governments, the World Bank and the UN – will need to be involved in these reform processes.

In the final analysis, this book has shown that CSR may bring benefits for society, but there are many limitations to voluntary activities. Too much focus on CSR may divert attention from broader political and economic solutions to societal challenges. If we want business to fulfil its potential for serving societal needs, the CSR approach is not enough.

Glossary

Accountability. Corporate accountability refers to having to answer for the consequences of a company's behaviour. Measures of accountability can range from social audits of a company and CSR reporting, to the legal liability for a company's actions. While there is no consensus on what corporate accountability should encompass, the term 'accountability' is usually understood to result in stricter obligations by companies in comparison with 'social responsibility'.

Civil society. Civil society is the sum of civic and social organisations and institutions, which form voluntarily to represent common interests. Civil society is not part of institutions of the state and commercial organisations. Non-governmental organisations such as Greenpeace and Amnesty International are considered part of civil society.

Equator Principles. The Equator Principles provide a voluntary set of guidelines for financial institutions to manage social and environmental issues related to project financing with project capital costs over US$10 million (see Box 3.1 for further information). **Website:** www.equator-principles.com

Extractive Industries Transparency Initiative (EITI). The EITI aims to improve governance in resource-rich countries through the full publication and verification of company payments and government revenues from oil, gas and mining (see Box 6.1 for further information). **Website:** www.eitransparency.org

Extractive Industries Transparency Initiative Plus Plus (EITI++). The EITI++ was launched by the World Bank in 2008 to help developing nations to manage their natural resource revenues. The EITI++ goes beyond the EITI by offering resource-rich countries World Bank assistance in designing natural resource contracts, monitoring operations, collecting taxes and, above all, spending natural resource revenues effectively.

Global Compact, see United Nations Global Compact.

Global Reporting Initiative (GRI). The GRI produces universal guidelines for measuring and reporting economic, environmental and social performance of organisations. The GRI Guidelines are the most common framework used in the world for environmental and social reporting, with over 1,500 companies having adopted the Guidelines. The GRI is an independent institution, but it collaborates with the UN Environment Programme and the *United Nations Global Compact* (see below). **Website:** www.globalreporting.org

International Finance Corporation (IFC). The IFC is an arm of the World Bank responsible for promoting the private sector in developing countries. It funds private sector projects, helps companies in the developing world to raise capital in international financial markets and provides advice and technical assistance to businesses and governments. The IFC directly funds many private businesses, for instance, by providing loans to companies in developing countries such as India, which have the potential of successfully expanding in the global market. **Website:** www.ifc.org

International Monetary Fund (IMF). The IMF was established in 1944 by a conference of forty-four governments at Bretton Woods in the United States. Its original aim was to supervise a system of so-called 'fixed' exchange rates between the world's currencies, but this system had collapsed by the 1970s. Today, the IMF's aims are to promote international monetary cooperation and exchange rate stability and to help member countries in dealing with temporary balance of payments difficulties. In return for a loan to a member country, the IMF can impose a set of conditions, including changes to the country's tax policy, changes to monetary policy, privatisation of formerly state-owned enterprises, currency devaluation, government spending cuts or removal of foreign investment restrictions. **Website:** www.imf.org

International Organization for Standardization (ISO). The ISO is a network of the national standards institutes of 157 countries (as of June 2008) and the world's largest developer of international standards. ISO standards are developed by technical committees of experts and they provide rules for good practice for a specified area. The ISO standards include the ISO 9000 series for quality management, the ISO 14000 series for environmental management and the ISO 26000 series for social responsibility (see below). However, the ISO itself does not certify that a company conforms to a specific standard. **Website:** www.iso.org

ISO 14000. ISO 14000 is a series of different environmental management standards developed by the International Organization for Standardization (ISO). The ISO 14001 standard is the principal standard used by firms and it addresses environmental management systems in general. Other standards of the ISO 14000 series address specific environmental aspects such as ISO 14031 (environmental performance evaluation), ISO 14044 (life cycle analysis) and ISO 14063 (environmental communication). **Website:** www.iso.org

ISO 26000. ISO 26000 is a new standard that addresses what companies need to do in order to operate in a socially responsible way. In contrast to standards for quality management and environmental management, the ISO 26000 contains guidelines – not requirements – and therefore cannot be used for certification of a company in the same way as ISO 9001 or ISO 14001 standards. **Website**: www.iso.org

Non-governmental organisation (NGO). An NGO is a not-for-profit pressure group which is independent of government.

Philanthropy. Philanthropy is the use of financial donations and expertise for the benefit of public causes. There is no consensus on whether corporate philanthropy should be considered a part of corporate social responsibility. There is a distinction between charity, which refers to the alleviation of human suffering, and philanthropy, which refers to a wider commitment to public benefit that seeks to address the causes of social problems such as poverty.

Sustainable development. According to the definition by the World Commission on Environment and Development, sustainable development means meeting the needs of the present without sacrificing the ability of future generations to meet their own needs.

United Nations Global Compact. The Global Compact is a UN initiative, which asks participating companies to subscribe to ten core principles in the areas of human rights, labour rights and the environment. The Global Compact network consists of several hundred companies, dozens of non-governmental organisations, major international labour federations and a number of UN agencies. **Website**: www.unglobalcompact.org

Voluntary Principles on Security and Human Rights. The Voluntary Principles were launched in 2000 by the governments of the United States and the UK in order to address security and human rights issues among extractive sector companies. The participating companies promise to support a set of general voluntary principles, which relate to three areas: (1) 'risk assessment' (e.g., identifying potential for violence); (2) 'interactions between companies and public security' (e.g., holding regular consultations with host governments and local communities on the impact of security arrangements); and (3) 'interactions between companies and private security' (e.g., individuals implicated in human rights abuses not to provide security protection for the company). **Website:** www.voluntaryprinciples.org

World Bank. Like the IMF, the World Bank was established in 1944 to help, principally, European nations recover from the devastation of the Second World War of 1939–45. Today, the World Bank is one of the world's largest sources of overseas development assistance, and its work focuses mainly on developing countries. The World Bank consists of several distinct institutions, including the *International Finance Corporation* (see above). It has initiated research and policy guidelines on Corporate Social Responsibility and sustainable development. In order to maximise the developmental potential of extractive industries, it has launched the Extractive Industries Transparency Initiative Plus Plus in 2008 (see above). **Website:** www.worldbank.org

World Business Council for Sustainable Development (WBCSD). The WBCSD is a CEO-led, global business association of about 200 companies dealing exclusively with sustainable development. The WBCSD provides a platform for companies to communicate with each other on sustainable development, share knowledge, experiences and best practices, and to represent common interests on social and environmental issues in dialogue with governments, non-governmental organisations and international organisations. **Website:** www.wbcsd.org

References

Acona. 2004. *Buying Your Way into Trouble? The Challenge of Responsible Supply Chain Management.* London: Insight Investment Management.

Adams, Ronald. 2005. Fast food, obesity, and tort reform: an examination of industry responsibility for public health. *Business and Society Review* 110 (3): 297–320.

Aguilera, Ruth V., Deborah E. Rupp, Cynthia A. Williams, and Jyoti Ganapathi. 2007. Putting the S back in corporate social responsibility: a multilevel theory of social change in organizations. *Academy of Management Review* 32 (3): 836–63.

Ahmad, Jaseem. 2006. From principles to practice: exploring corporate social responsibility in Pakistan. *Journal of Corporate Citizenship* (24): 115–29.

Akhurst, Mark, Jeff Morgheim, and Rachel Lewis. 2003. Greenhouse gas emissions trading in BP. *Energy Policy* 31 (7): 657–63.

Alt, James E., and David Dreyer Lassen. 2006a. Fiscal transparency, political parties, and debt in OECD countries. *European Economic Review* 50 (6): 1403–39.

Alt, James E., and David Dreyer Lassen. 2006b. Transparency, political polarization, and political budget cycles in OECD countries. *American Journal of Political Science* 50 (3): 530–50.

Amaeshi, Kenneth, and Bongo Adi. 2007. Reconstructing the corporate social responsibility construct in Utlish. *Business Ethics: A European Review* 16 (1): 3–18.

Amaeshi, Kenneth, Bongo Adi, Chris Ogbechie, and Olufemi Amao. 2006. Corporate social responsibility in Nigeria: Western mimicry or indigenous influences? *Journal of Corporate Citizenship* (24): 83–99.

Amaeshi, Kenneth, and Andrew Crane. 2006. Stakeholder engagement: a mechanism for sustainable aviation. *Corporate Social Responsibility and Environmental Management* 13 (5): 245–60.

Andriof, Jörg, and Sandra Waddock. 2002. Unfolding stakeholder engagement. In *Unfolding Stakeholder Thinking: Theory, Responsibility and Engagement*, ed. J. Andriof, S. Waddock, B. Husted and S. S. Rahman. Sheffield: Greenleaf, 19–42.

Anonymous. 1997. BP at war. *The Economist*, 19 July, 32–4.

2001. Nigeria and Shell – helping, but not developing. *The Economist*, 12 May.

Aslaksen, Iulie, and Terje Synnestvedt. 2003. Ethical investment and the incentives for corporate environmental protection and social responsibility. *Corporate Social Responsibility and Environmental Management* 10 (4): 212–23.

Austin, D., and A. Sauer. 2002. *Changing Oil: Emerging Environmental Risks and Shareholder Value in the Oil and Gas Industry*. Washington, DC: World Resources Institute.

Baena, César E. 1999. *The Policy Process in a Petro-State – An Analysis of PDVSA's Internationalisation Strategy*. Aldershot: Ashgate.

Bansal, Pratima. 2005. Evolving sustainably: a longitudinal study of corporate sustainable development. *Strategic Management Journal* 26 (3): 197–218.

Baron, David P. 2001. Private politics, corporate social responsibility and integrated strategy. *Journal of Economics & Management Strategy* 10: 7–45.

2007. Corporate social responsibility and social entrepreneurship. *Journal of Economics & Management Strategy* 16 (3): 683–717.

Barrientos, Stephanie, and Sally Smith. 2007. Do workers benefit from ethical trade? Assessing codes of labour practice in global production systems. *Third World Quarterly* 28 (4): 713–29.

Baskin, Jeremy. 2006. Corporate Responsibility in emerging markets. *Journal of Corporate Citizenship* 24: 29–47.

Bell, Joseph, Teresa Faria, Macartan Humphreys, Peter Rosenblum and Martin E. Sandbu. 2004. *Sao Tome and Principe Oil Revenue Management Law – Oil-Revenue Management Team of the Columbia University Consulting Group to H.E. The President of Sao Tome and Principe*. New York: The Earth Institute, Center on Globalization and Sustainable Development, Columbia University.

Bendell, Jem, ed. 2000. *Terms for Endearment – Business, NGOs and Sustainable Development*. Sheffield: Greenleaf.

Bennett, Craig, and Helen Burley. 2005. Corporate accountability: an NGO perspective. In *Research Handbook on Corporate Legal Responsibility*, ed. S. Tully. Cheltenham: Edward Elgar, 372–94.

Besley, Timothy, and Andrea Prat. 2006. Handcuffs for the grabbing hand? Media capture and government accountability. *American Economic Review* 96 (3): 720–36.

Bhatnagar, Smita, and Mark A. Cohen. 1997. *The Impact of Environmental Regulation on Innovation: A Panel Data Study*. Nashville, TN: Owen Graduate School of Management, Vanderbilt University.

Bielak, Debby, Sheila Bonini and Jeremy Oppenheim. 2007. CEOs on strategy and social issues. *McKinsey Quarterly*, October, available at www.mckinseyquarterly.com/strategy/ceos_on_strategy_and_social_issues_2056.

Blowfield, Michael. 2005. Corporate social responsibility: reinventing the meaning of development? *International Affairs* 81 (3): 515–24.

2007. Reasons to be cheerful? What we know about CSR's impact. *Third World Quarterly* 28 (4): 683–96.

Blowfield, Michael, and Jedrzej George Frynas. 2005. Editorial: setting new agendas – critical perspectives on corporate social responsibility in the developing world. *International Affairs* 81 (3): 499–513.

Blowfield, Michael, and Alan Murray. 2008. *Corporate Responsibility – A Critical Introduction*. Oxford: Oxford University Press.

Bonvin, Jean-Michel. 2007. Corporate social responsibility in a context of permanent restructuring: a case study from the Swiss metal-working sector. *Corporate Governance: An International Review* 15 (1): 36–44.

Bowen, Michael G., and F. Clark Power. 1993. The moral manager: communicative ethics and the *Exxon Valdez* disaster. *Business Ethics Quarterly* 3 (2): 97–115.

Bowie, Norman. 1998. A Kantian theory of capitalism. *Business Ethics Quarterly* 1 (1): 37–60.

Bremmers, Harry, Onno Omta, Ron Kemp, and Derk-Jan Haverkamp. 2007. Do stakeholder groups influence environmental management system development in the Dutch agri-food sector? *Business Strategy and the Environment* 16: 214–31.

Brower, Derek. 2007. Back to petroleum. *Petroleum Economist*, November, 6–7.

Campbell, John L. 2007. Why would corporations behave in socially responsible ways? An institutional theory of corporate social responsibility. *Academy of Management Review* 32 (3): 946–67.

Carroll, Archie B. 1991. The pyramid of corporate social responsibility: Toward the moral management of organizational stakeholders. *Business Horizons* 34 (4): 39–48.

2004. Managing ethically with global stakeholders: a present and future challenge. *Academy of Management Executive* 18 (2): 114–19.

Cassel, Douglass. 2001. Human rights and business responsibilities in the global marketplace. *Business Ethics Quarterly* 11 (2): 261–74.

Catholic Relief Services. 2003. *Bottom of the Barrel – Africa's Oil Boom and the Poor.* Baltimore, MD: Catholic Relief Services.

Centre for Civic Initiatives, Committee for the Protection of Oil Workers Rights, CEE Bankwatch Network, Green Alternative, Kurdish Human Rights Project, PLATFORM and Urgewald. 2005. *Baku-Tbilisi-Ceyhan Oil Pipeline: Human Rights, Social and Environmental Impacts (Georgia Section) – Final Report of Fact Finding Mission 16–18 September 2005.* Baku: Centre for Civic Initiatives and six other organisations.

Chan, Anita. 2005. Recent trends in Chinese labour issues: signs of change. *China Perspectives* 57: 23–31.

Chen, Matthew E. 2007. *National Oil Companies and Corporate Citizenship: A Survey of Transnational Policy and Practice.* Houston, TX: The James A. Baker III Institute for Public Policy, Rice University.

Christian Aid. 2004. *Behind the Mask: The Real Face of Corporate Social Responsibility.* London: Christian Aid.

Ciulla, Joanne B. 1991. Why is business talking about ethics? Reflections on foreign conversations. *California Management Review* 34 (1): 67–86.

Clark, Ann Marie. 1995. Non-governmental organizations and their influence on international society. *Journal of International Affairs* 48 (2): 507–25.

Clark, R. B., ed. 1982. *The Long-term Effects of Oil Pollution on Marine Populations, Communities and Ecosystems.* London: The Royal Society.

Clarkson, M. B. E. 1995. A stakeholder framework for analyzing and evaluating corporate social performance. *Academy of Management Review* 20: 92–117.

Collier, Paul, and Anke Hoeffler. 1998. On the economic causes of civil war. *Oxford Economic Papers* 50: 563–73.

2000. *Greed and Grievance in Civil War.* Policy Research Working Paper 2355. Washington, DC: World Bank.

Colvin, Geoff. 2007. The defiant one. *Fortune*, 30 April.

Cordato, Roy. 2004. Toward an Austrian theory of environmental economics. *Quarterly Journal of Austrian Economics* 7 (1): 3–16.

Corden, W. M. 1984. Booming sector and Dutch disease economics: survey and consolidation. *Oxford Economic Papers* **36**: 359–80.

Crane, Andrew. 2000. Facing the backlash: green marketing and strategic reorientation in the 1990s. *Journal of Strategic Marketing* **8** (3): 277–96.

Cresswell, Jeremy. 2008. The power of the NOCs. *World Oil* (May): 135–41.

Davis, Ann, Amir Efrati, Matthew Dalton and Guy Chazan. 2007. BP settles charges, submits to watchdogs. *Wall Street Journal*, 26 October, A3.

Deakin, Simon, and Richard Hobbs. 2007. False dawn for CSR? Shifts in regulatory policy and the response of the corporate and financial sectors in Britain. *Corporate Governance: An International Review* **15** (1): 68–76.

Department for International Development. 2001. *Socially Responsible Business Team Strategy: April 2001–March 2004*. London: DfID.

DesJardins, Joe. 1998. Corporate environmental responsibility. *Journal of Business Ethics* **17** (8): 825–38.

DiMaggio, P. J., and W. W. Powell. 1983. The iron cage revisited: institutional isomorphism and collective rationality in organizational fields. *American Sociological Review* **48**: 147–60.

Dixon, Sarah E. A., and Anne Clifford. 2007. Ecopreneurship – a new approach to managing the triple bottom line. *Journal of Organizational Change Management* **20** (3): 326–45.

Doh, Jonathan P., and Terrence R. Guay. 2006. Corporate social responsibility, public policy, and NGO activism in Europe and the United States: an institutional-stakeholder perspective. *Journal of Management Studies* **43** (1): 47–73.

Donaldson, L., and J. H. Davis. 1991. Stewardship theory or agency theory: CEO governance and shareholder returns. *Australian Journal of Management* **16**: 49–64.

Donaldson, Thomas, and Lee E. Preston. 1995. The stakeholder theory of the corporation: Concepts, evidence, and implications. *Academy of Management Review* **20** (1): 65–91.

Drumwright, Minette E. 1994. Socially responsible organizational buying: environmental concern as a noneconomic buying criterion. *Journal of Marketing* **58** (3): 1–19.

Economist Intelligence Unit. 2006. *Country Profile 2006 – Azerbaijan*. London: Economist Intelligence Unit.

Elbadawi, Ibrahim, and Nicholas Sambanis. 2000. Why are there so many civil wars in Africa? Understanding and preventing violent conflict. *Journal of African Economies* **9** (3): 244–69.

Ellerman, D. 2001. *Helping People Help Themselves: Toward a Theory of Autonomy-compatible Help.* Washington, DC: World Bank.

Emmelhainz, Margaret A., and Ronald J. Adams. 1999. The apparel industry response to 'sweatshop' concerns: a review and analysis of codes of conduct. *Journal of Supply Chain Management* 35 (3): 51–7.

Encyclopedia Britannica. 2004. *Encyclopedia Britannica: Year in Review 2003.* Chicago, IL: Encyclopedia Britannica.

Estrada, Javier, Kristian Tangen and Helge Ole Bergesen. 1997. *Environmental Challenges Confronting the Oil Industry.* New York: Wiley.

European Social Investment Forum. 2006. *2006 European SRI Study.* Paris: Eurosif-European Social Investment Forum.

Faber, Malte, John Proops, Stefan Speck and Frank Jöst. 1999. *Capital and Time in Ecological Economics: Neo-Austrian Modelling.* Cheltenham: Edward Elgar.

Fabig, Heike, and Richard Boele. 1999. The changing nature of NGO activity in a globalizing world: pushing the corporate responsibility agenda. *IDS Bulletin* 30 (3): 58–87.

Fig, David. 2005. Manufacturing amnesia: CSR in South Africa. *International Affairs* 81 (3): 599–619.

Freeman, Bennett. 2001. Drilling for common ground. *Foreign Policy* (July/August): 50.

Freeman, Richard E. 1984. *Strategic Management – A Stakeholder Approach.* Boston: Pitman.

1994. The politics of stakeholder theory: some future directions. *Business Ethics Quarterly* 4 (4): 409–21.

Freeman, Richard E. and David Reed. 1983. Stockholders and stakeholders: a new perspective on corporate governance. *California Management Review* 25 (3): 88–106.

Friedman, Milton. 1962. *Capitalism and Freedom.* Chicago: University of Chicago Press.

Frynas, Jedrzej George. 1998. Political instability and business: focus on Shell in Nigeria. *Third World Quarterly* 19 (3): 457–79.

2000. *Oil in Nigeria: Conflict and Litigation between Oil Companies and Village Communities.* Münster/Hamburg: LIT.

2001. Corporate and state responses to anti-oil protests in the Niger Delta. *African Affairs* 100: 27–54.

2003a. Global monitor: Royal Dutch/Shell. *New Political Economy* 8 (2): 275–85.

2003b. The transnational garment industry in South and South-East Asia. In *Transnational Corporations and Human Rights*, edited by J. G. Frynas and S. Pegg. Basingstoke: Palgrave, 162–87.

2004. The oil boom in Equatorial Guinea. *African Affairs* 103 (413): 527–46.

2005. The false developmental promise of corporate social responsibility: evidence from multinational oil companies. *International Affairs* 81 (3): 581–98.

2006. Editorial: corporate social responsibility in emerging economies. *Journal of Corporate Citizenship* (24): 16–19.

2008. Corporate social responsibility and international development: critical assessment. Corporate Governance: *An International Review* 16 (4): 274–81.

Frynas, Jedrzej George, Kamel Mellahi, and Geoffrey Pigman. 2006. First mover advantages in international business and firm-specific political resources. *Strategic Management Journal* 27: 321–45.

Frynas, Jedrzej George, and Manuel Paulo. 2007. A new scramble for African oil? Historical, political, and business perspectives. *African Affairs* 106 (423): 229–51.

Frynas, Jedrzej George and Geoffrey Wood. 2001. Oil and war in Angola. *Review of African Political Economy* 28 (90): 587–606.

Gelb, Alan et al. 1988. *Oil Windfalls: Blessing or curse*. New York: Oxford University Press.

Gelos, Gaston, and Shang-Jin Wei. 2005. Transparency and international portfolio holdings. *Journal of Finance* 60 (6): 2987–3020.

Getz, Kathleen A. 1993. Selecting corporate political tactics. In *Corporate Political Agency: The Construction of Competition in Public Affairs*, edited by B. M. Mitnick. Newbury Park, CA: Sage, 242–73.

Glennerster, Rachel, and Yongseok Shin. 2003. *Is Transparency Good for You, and Can the IMF Help?* Washington, DC: International Monetary Fund.

Global Witness. 2004. *Time for Transparency – Coming Clean on Oil, Mining and Gas Revenues*. London: Global Witness.

Gould, John A. and Matthew S. Winters. 2007. An obsolescing bargain in Chad: shifts in leverage between the government and the World Bank. *Business and Politics* 9 (2): 1–34.

Gouldson, Andy and Rory Sullivan. 2007. Corporate environmentalism: tracing the links between policies and performance using corporate reports and public registers. *Business Strategy and the Environment* 16 (1): 1–11.

Graafland, Johan J. 2002. Sourcing ethics in the textile sector: the case of C&A. *Business Ethics: A European Review* 11 (3): 282–94.

Gueterbock, Rob. 2004. Greenpeace campaign case study – StopEsso. *Journal of Consumer Behaviour* 3 (3): 265–71.

Gulbrandsen, Lars H. and Arild Moe. 2005. Oil company CSR collaboration in 'new' petro-states. *Journal of Corporate Citizenship* (20): 1–12.

2007. BP in Azerbaijan: a test case of the potential and limits of the CSR agenda? *Third World Quarterly* 28 (4): 813–30.

Gylfason, Thorvaldur. 2001. Natural resources, education and economic development. *European Economic Review* 45: 847–59.

Hamann, Ralph, Tagbo Agbazue, Paul Kapelus and Anders Hein. 2005. Universalizing corporate social responsibility? South African challenges to the International Organization for Standardization's new social responsibility standard. *Business and Society Review* 110 (1): 1–19.

Hargreaves, Steve. 2008. BP, GM see hydrogen in their future. *CNNMoney*, 5 March.

Hart, S. 1995. A natural resource-based view of the firm. *Academy of Management Review* 20: 986–1014.

Henderson Global Investors. 2005. *The Carbon 100 – Quantifying the Carbon Emissions, Intensities and Exposures of the FTSE 100.* London: Henderson Global Investors.

Henriques, Adrian. 2007. *Corporate Truth – The Limits to Transparency.* London: Earthscan.

Heywood, Andrew. 2002. *Politics*, 2nd edn. Houndmills: Palgrave.

Hill, C. W. L, and T. M. Jones. 1992. Stakeholder-agency theory. *Journal of Management Studies* 29 (2): 131–54.

Hillman, Amy J., and Michael A. Hitt. 1999. Corporate political strategy formulation: a model of approach, participation, and strategy decisions. *Academy of Management Review* 24 (4): 825–42.

Hoffman, Andrew. 2004. Winning the greenhouse gas game. *Harvard Business Review* 82 (4): 20–1.

Hojman, D. E. 2002. The political economy of Chile's fast economic growth: an Olsonian interpretation. *Public Choice* 111 (1/2): 155–78.

Hussain, Syed Salman. 1999. The ethics of 'going green': the corporate social responsibility debate. *Business Strategy and the Environment* 8 (4): 203–10.

Hyne, Norman J. 1995. *Nontechnical Guide to Petroleum Geology, Exploration, Drilling and Production.* Tulsa, OK: PennWell.

Innovest, and Environment Agency. 2004. *Corporate Environmental Governance: A Study into the Influence of Environmental Governance on Financial Performance*. London: Environment Agency.

International Council on Human Rights Policy. 2002. *Beyond Voluntarism – Human Rights and the Developing International Legal Obligations of Companies*. Geneva: International Council on Human Rights Policy.

International Oil Pollution Compensation Funds, ed. 2004. *The IOPC Funds' 25 Years of Compensating Victims of Oil Pollution Incidents*. London: International Oil Pollution Compensation Funds.

IPIECA, OGP and UNEP. 2002. *Industry As a Partner for Sustainable Development – Oil and Gas*. London: International Petroleum Industry Environmental Conservation Association, International Association of Oil and Gas Producers and United Nations Environment Programme.

James, Tom. 2006. Oil risk management. Seminar presentation given at Middlesex University Business School, Department of Economics and Statistics, 8 November.

Jawahar, I. and G. McLaughlin. 2001. Toward a descriptive stakeholder theory: an organizational life cycle approach. *Academy of Management Review* **26** (3): 397–414.

Jayne, Michael Ross and Glynn Skerratt. 2003. Socially responsible investment in the UK – criteria that are used to evaluate suitability. *Corporate Social Responsibility and Environmental Management* **10** (1): 1–11.

Jenkins, Rhys. 2005. Globalization, corporate social responsibility and poverty. *International Affairs* **81** (3): 525–40.

Jenkins, Rhys, Ruth Pearson and Gill Seyfang, eds. 2002. *Corporate Responsibility and Labour Rights: Codes of Conduct in the Global Economy*. London: Earthscan.

Jennings, P. and P. Zandbergen. 1995. Ecologically sustainable organizations: an institutional approach. *Academy of Management Review* **20**: 1015–52.

Jones, Meredith , Shelley Marshall and Richard Mitchell. 2007. Corporate social responsibility and the management of labour in two Australian mining industry companies. *Corporate Governance: An International Review* **15** (1): 57–67.

Kamp, Annette and Peter Hagedorn-Rasmussen. 2004. Diversity management in a Danish context: towards a multicultural or segregated working life. *Economic and Industrial Democracy* **25** (4): 525–54.

Karl, Terry L. 1997. *The Paradox of Plenty: Oil Booms and Petro-States*. Berkeley: University of California Press.

2005. Understanding the resource curse. In *Covering Oil*, ed. S. Tsalik and A. Schiffrin. New York: Open Society Institute, 21–30.

Keen, David. 1998. *The Economic Functions of Violence in Civil Wars*. Adelphi Paper 320. Oxford: Oxford University Press.

Keim, Gerald D. and Carl P. Zeithaml. 1986. Corporate political strategy and legislative decision making: a review and contingency approach. *Academy of Management Review* 11 (4): 828–43.

Knight, W. D., N. C. Alagoa and D. Von Kemedi. 2000. Akassa: a new approach to the problems of the Niger Delta. Paper read at SPE International Conference on Health, Safety and the Environment in Oil and Gas Exploration and Production, 26–28 June, at Stavanger, Norway.

Knott, David. 1999. Improving viability of renewable energy beckons petroleum firms' investment. *Oil & Gas Journal* (13 December): 127–9.

Kojucharov, Nikola. 2007. Poverty, petroleum and policy intervention: lessons from the Chad–Cameroon Pipeline. *Review of African Political Economy* 34 (113): 477–96.

Kolk, Ans and Rob van Tulder. 2006. Poverty alleviation as business strategy? Evaluating commitments of frontrunner multinational corporations. *World Development* 34 (5): 789–801.

Kolk, Ans, Seb Walhain and Susanne van de Wateringen. 2001. Environmental reporting by the *Fortune* Global 250: exploring the influence of nationality and sector. *Business Strategy and the Environment* 10 (1): 15–28.

Korhonen, Jouni. 2002. The dominant economics paradigm and corporate social responsibility. *Corporate Social Responsibility and Environmental Management* 9 (1): 67–80.

KPMG. 2005. *International Survey of Corporate Responsibility Reporting*. Amsterdam: University of Amsterdam and KPMG Global Sustainability Services.

Langtry, B. 1994. Stakeholders and the moral responsibilities of business. *Business Ethics Quarterly* 4: 431–43.

Lanjouw, Jean Olson and Ashoka Mody. 1996. Innovation and the international diffusion of environmentally responsive technology. *Research Policy* 25: 549–71.

Leite, Carlos, and Jens Weidmann. 1999. *Does Mother Nature Corrupt? Natural Resources, Corruption and Economic Growth*. Washington, DC: International Monetary Fund.

Levenstein, Charles, and John Wooding. 2005. Introduction: oil and the contradictions of development. In *Corporate Social Responsibility*

Failures in the Oil Industry, ed. C. Woolfson and M. Beck. Amityville, NY: Baywood, v–vii.

Levy, David L. and Ans Kolk. 2002. Strategic responses to global climate change: conflicting pressures on multinationals in the oil industry. *Business and Politics* **4** (3): 275–300.

Lewin, Peter and Steven E. Phelan. 1999. Firms, strategies, and resources: contributions from Austrian economics. *Quarterly Journal of Austrian Economics* **2** (2): 3–18.

Lockett, Andy, Jeremy Moon and Wayne Wisser. 2006. Corporate social responsibility in management research: focus, nature, salience and sources of influence. *Journal of Management Studies* **43** (1): 115–36.

Lounsbury, Michael, Marc Ventresca and Paul Hirsch. 2003. Social movements, field frames and industry emergence: a cultural-political perspective on US recycling. *Socio-Economic Review* **1** (1): 71–104.

Macalister, Terry. 2007. Big oil lets sun set on renewables. *Guardian*, 11 December.

   2008. BP hints at sale of alternative energy business. *Guardian*, 27 February.

MacDonald, Kate. 2007. Globalising justice within coffee supply chains? Fair Trade, Starbucks and the transformation of supply chain governance. *Third World Quarterly* **28** (4): 793–812.

McGee, John. 1998. Commentary on 'Corporate strategies and environmental regulations: an organizing framework' by A. M. Rugman and A. Verbeke. *Strategic Management Journal* **19** (4): 377–87.

Mackey, Alison, Tyson B. Mackey and Jay B. Barney. 2007. Corporate social responsibility and firm performance: investor preferences and corporate strategies. *Academy of Management Review* **32** (3): 817–83.

McKinsey & Company. 2007. *Assessing the Impact of Societal Issues: A McKinsey Global Survey*, available at www.mckinseyquarterly.com/assessing_the_impact_of_societal_issues_a_mckinsey_global_survey_2077.

McLaren, Duncan. 2004. Global stakeholders: corporate accountability and investor engagement. *Corporate Governance: An International Review* **12** (2): 191–201.

McWilliams, Abagail and Donald S. Siegel. 2001. Corporate social responsibility: a theory of the firm perspective. *Academy of Management Review* **26**: 117–27.

McWilliams, Abagail, Donald S. Siegel, and Patrick M. Wright. 2006. Guest editors' introduction – corporate social responsibility: strategic implications. *Journal of Management Studies* **43** (1): 1–18.

McWilliams, Abagail, D. D. Van Fleet and K. D. Cory. 2002. Raising rivals' costs through political strategy: an extension of resource-based theory. *Journal of Management Studies* 39 (5): 707–23.

Malone, Thomas W. 2004. Bringing the market inside. *Harvard Business Review* 82 (4): 106–14.

Marcel, Valerie and John V. Mitchell. 2005. *Oil Titans: National Oil Companies in the Middle East*. Washington, DC: Brookings Institution.

Margolis, Joshua D. and James P. Walsh. 2003. Misery loves companies: rethinking social initiatives by business. *Administrative Science Quarterly* 48: 268–305.

Matten, Dirk and Andrew Crane. 2005. Corporate citizenship: towards an extended theoretical conceptualization. *Academy of Management Review* 30 (1): 166–79.

Mensah, Thomas. 2004. The IOPC funds: how it all started. In *The IOPC Funds' 25 Years of Compensating Victims of Oil Pollution Incidents*. London: International Oil Pollution Compensation Funds, 45–9.

Messiant, Christine. 2001. The Eduardo dos Santos Foundation: or, how Angola's regime is taking over civil society. *African Affairs* 100: 287–309.

Meyer, J. W. and B. Rowan. 1977. Institutionalized organizations: formal structure as myth and ceremony. *American Journal of Sociology* 83: 340–63.

Mises, Ludwig von. 1940. *Nationalökonomie – Theorie des Handelns und Wirtschaftens*. Genf: Editions Union Genf.

1963. *Human Action*, 3rd edn. Chicago: Yale University Press.

1969. *Theory and History: An Interpretation of Social and Economic Evolution*. New York: Arlington House.

Mitchell, Ronald K., Bradley R. Agle and Donna J. Wood. 1997. Toward a theory of stakeholder identification and salience. *Academy of Management Review* 22: 853–86.

Mitnick, Barry M., ed. 1993. *Corporate Political Agency: The Construction of Competition in Public Affairs*. Newbury Park, CA: Sage.

MOL Group. 2007. *Sustainable Development Report 2006*. Budapest: MOL Group.

Moon, Jeremy. 2004. *Government As a Driver of Corporate Social Responsibility: The UK in Comparative Perspective*. ICCSR Research Papers Series 20–2004. Nottingham: International Centre for Corporate Social Responsibility, Nottingham University Business School.

Muttitt, Greg and James Marriott. 2002. *Some Common Concerns – Imagining BP's Azerbaijan–Georgia–Turkey Pipelines System*. London: Platform.

Newell, Peter and Jedrzej George Frynas. 2007. Beyond corporate social responsibility? Business, poverty and social justice. *Third World Quarterly* **28** (4): 669–81.

Newell, Peter and Ana Muro. 2006. Corporate social and environmental responsibility in Argentina. *Journal of Corporate Citizenship* **24**: 49–68.

Newell, Peter and Joanna Wheeler. 2006. *Rights, Resources and the Politics of Accountability*. London: Zed Books.

Nicholls, Tom. 2007. Alternative realities. *Petroleum Economist* (March) 4–6.

North, D. C. and R. P. Thomas. 1973. *The Rise of the Western World: A New Economic History*. Cambridge: Cambridge University Press.

O'Dwyer, Brendan. 2005. The construction of a social account: a case study in an overseas aid agency. *Accounting, Organizations and Society* **30** (3): 279–96.

OECD. 2000. *Improving the Effectiveness of Aid Systems: The Case of Mali*. Paris: OECD.

Olander, Stefan. 2007. Stakeholder impact analysis in construction project management. *Construction Management and Economics* **25** (3): 277–87.

Olson, Mancur. 1965. *The Logic of Collective Action – Public Goods and the Theory of Groups*. Cambridge, MA: Harvard University Press.

Owen, David L., Tracey A. Swift, Christopher Humphrey and Mary Bowerman. 2000. The new social audits: accountability, managerial capture or the agenda of social champions? *European Accounting Review* **9** (1): 81–98.

Paine, L., R. Deshpande, J. D. Margolis and K. E. Bettcher. 2005. Up to code: does your company's conduct meet world-class standards? *Harvard Business Review* **83** (12): 122–33.

Palazzo, Guido, and Ulf Richter. 2005. CSR business as usual? The case of the tobacco industry. *Journal of Business Ethics* **61** (4): 387–401.

Parkinson, John. 1999. The socially responsible company. In *Human Rights Standards and the Responsibility of Transnational Corporations*, ed. M. K. Addo. The Hague: Kluwer Law International, 49–62.

Pegg, Scott. 2003. An emerging market for the new millennium: transnational corporations and human rights. In *Transnational Corporations and Human Rights*, ed. J. G. Frynas and S. Pegg. London: Palgrave, 1–32.

2006. Can policy intervention beat the resource curse? Evidence from the Chad–Cameroon pipeline project. *African Affairs* **105** (418): 1–25.

Phillips, Robert A. 1997. Stakeholder theory and a principle of fairness. *Business Ethics Quarterly* 7 (1): 51–66.

2003. *Stakeholder Theory and Organizational Ethics.* San Francisco, CA: Barrett-Koehler.

Phillips, Robert A. and Joshua D. Margolis. 1999. Toward an ethics of organizations. *Business Ethics Quarterly* 9 (4): 619–38.

Porter, Michael E. 1991. America's green strategy. *Scientific American* 264: 168.

Porter, Michael E. and Mark R. Kramer. 2006. Strategy and society – the link between competitive advantage and corporate social responsibility. *Harvard Business Review* (December): 78–92.

Porter, Michael E. and Claas van der Linde. 1995. Green and competitive: ending the stalemate. *Harvard Business Review* 73 (5): 120–34.

Prasad, Ajit. 2005. CSR as Nash equilibrium. *Journal of Management Research* 5 (2): 59–71.

Publish What You Pay and Revenue Watch Institute. 2006. *Eye on EITI – Civil Society Perspectives and Recommendations on the Extractive Industries Transparency Initiative.* London/New York: Publish What You Pay and Revenue Watch Institute.

Raeburn, Paul. 1999. It's time to put the *Valdez* behind us. *Business Week,* 29 March.

Ray, Dennis M. 1972. Corporations and American foreign relations. *Annals of the American Academy of Political and Social Science* 403 (September): 80–92.

Reed, Stanley. 2007. The problem's not peak oil, it's politics. *Business Week,* 9 July.

Rice, David. 2002. Human rights strategies for corporations. *Business Ethics: A European Review* 11 (2): 134–6.

Rice, Tony and Paula Owen. 1999. *Decommissioning the Brent Spar.* London: E & FN Spon.

Roberts, Peter W. and Kathleen M. Eisenhardt. 2003. Austrian insights on strategic organization: from market insights to implications for firms. *Strategic Organization* 1 (3): 345–52.

Rose-Ackermann, Susan. 1999. *Corruption and Government.* Cambridge: Cambridge University Press.

Ross, Michael L. 1999. The political economy of the resource curse. *World Politics* 51 (2): 297–322.

2001. Does oil hinder democracy? *World Politics* 53 (3): 325–61.

Rothbard, Murray N. 1962. *Man, Economy, and State: A Treatise on Economic Principles,* 2 vols. Princeton: D. Van Nostrand Company.

Rowlands, I. H. 2000. Beauty and the beast? BP's and Exxon's positions on global climate change. *Environment and Planning C* 18: 339–54.

Ruggie, John. 2007. *Business and Human Rights: Mapping International Standards of Responsibility and Accountability for Corporate Acts – Report of the Special Representative of the Secretary-General (SRSG) on the Issue of Human Rights and Transnational Corporations and Other Business Enterprises.* Geneva: United Nations.

Russo, Michael V. and Paul A. Fouts. 1997. A resource-based perspective on corporate environmental performance and profitability. *Academy of Management Journal* 40 (3): 534–59.

Sachs, Jeffrey D. and Andrew M. Warner. 1999. The big push, natural resource booms and growth. *Journal of Development Economics* 59 (1): 43–76.

2001. Natural resources and economic development: the curse of natural resources. *European Economic Review* 45: 827–38.

Saha, Monica and Geoffrey Darnton. 2005. Green companies or green companies: are companies really green, or are they pretending to be? *Business and Society Review* 110 (2): 117–58.

Sarraf, Maria and Moortaza Jiwanji. 2001. *Beating the Resource Curse: The Case of Botswana.* Washington, DC: World Bank.

Schattschneider, E. E. 1935. *Politics, Pressures and the Tariff – A Study of Free Enterprise in Pressure Politics As Shown in the 1939–1930 Revision of the Tariff.* New York: Prentice Hall.

Scholtens, Bert. 2006. Finance as a driver of corporate social responsibility. *Journal of Business Ethics* (68): 19–33.

Schumacher, E. F. 1973. *Small Is Beautiful: Economics As If People Mattered.* New York: Harper and Row.

Scott, Richard W. 2001. *Institutions and Organizations*, 2nd edn. Thousand Oaks, CA: Sage Publications.

Screpanti, Ernesto and Stefano Zamagni. 1993. *An Outline of the History of Economic Thought.* Oxford: Clarendon Press.

Sekhar, R. C. 2002. *Ethical Choices in Business.* Delhi: Response Books.

Shaffer, Brian and Amy J. Hillman. 2000. The development of business – government strategies by diversified firms. *Strategic Management Journal* 21 (2): 175–90.

Shankleman, Jill. 2006. *Managing Natural Resource Wealth.* Washington, DC: United States Institute of Peace.

Sharma, Sanjay and Harrie Vredenburg. 1998. Proactive corporate environmental strategy and the development of competitively valuable organizational capabilities. *Strategic Management Journal* 19 (8): 729–53.

Shell Nigeria. 2007. *Annual Report 2006 – People and the Environment.* London: Shell Visual Media Services.

Shi, Min and Jakob Svensson. 2002. *Conditional Political Budget Cycles.* Discussion Paper 3352. London: Centre for Economic Policy Research.

Shultz, Jim. 2004. *Follow the Money – A Guide to Monitoring Budgets and Oil and Gas Revenues.* New York: Open Society Institute.

Skjærseth, Jon Birger and Tora Skodvin. 2003. *Climate Change and the Oil Industry: Common Problem, Varying Strategies.* Manchester/New York: Manchester University Press.

Skjærseth, Jon Birger, Kristian Tangen, Philip Swanson, Atle Christer Christiansen, Arild Moe and Leiv Lunde. 2004. *Limits to Corporate Social Responsibility: A Comparative Study of Four Major Oil Companies.* Lysaker, Norway: Fridtjof Nansen Institute.

Smeltzer, Larry and Marianne Jennings. 2006. Why an international code of business ethics would be good for business. *Journal of Business Ethics* 63 (2): 57–66.

Spar, Debora. 1998. The spotlight and the bottom line: how multinationals export human rights. *Foreign Affairs* 77 (2): 7–12.

Spear, Roger. 2006. Social entrepreneurship: a different model? *International Journal of Social Economics* 33 (5/6): 399–410.

Stark, Andrew. 1993. What's the matter with business ethics? *Harvard Business Review* 71 (3): 38–48.

Stevens, Paul. 2005. Resource curse and how to avoid it. *Journal of Energy and Development* 31 (1): 1–20.

Stoneley, Robert. 1995. *Introduction to Petroleum Exploration for Non-geologists.* Oxford: Oxford University Press.

SustainAbility. 2001. *Buried treasure: Uncovering the Business Case for Corporate Sustainability.* London: SustainAbility and United Nations Environment Programme.

  2002. *Developing Value: The Business Case for Sustainability in Emerging Markets.* London: SustainAbility, International Finance Corporation and Ethos.

Svendsen, Ann C. and Myriam Laberge. 2005. Convening stakeholder networks: a new way of thinking, being and engaging. *Journal of Corporate Citizenship* (19): 91–104.

Tallontire, Anne. 2007. Who regulates the agri-food chain? Towards a framework for understanding private standards initiatives. *Third World Quarterly* 28 (4): 775–91.

Tétreault, Mary Ann. 1995. *The Kuwait Petroleum Corporation and the Economics of the New World Order*. Westport, CT: Quorum.

Thompson-Feraru, A. 1974. Transnational political interests and the global environment. *International Organization* **28**: 31–60.

Thornton, Philip. 2004. Exposed: BP, its pipeline, and an environmental timebomb. *The Independent*, 26 June, 1, 6.

Transparency International. 2006. *Global Corruption Report 2006*. London: Pluto Press.

2008. *Promoting Revenue Transparency – 2008 Report on Revenue Transparency of Oil and Gas Companies*. Berlin: Transparency International.

Tsai, Philip C. F., C. Rosa Yeh, Shu-Ling Wu and Ing-Chung Huang. 2005. An empirical test of stakeholder influence strategy models: evidence from business downsizing in Taiwan. *International Journal of Human Resource Management* **16** (10): 1862–85.

United Nations Conference on Trade and Development. 2007. *World Investment Report – Transnational Corporations, Extractive Industries and Development*. New York and Geneva: United Nations.

US Agency for International Development. 2003. *The Global Development Alliance – Expanding the Impact of Foreign Assistance through Public-Private Alliances*. Washington, DC: USAID.

Usui, N. 1996. Policy adjustments to the oil boom and their evaluation: the Dutch disease in Indonesia. *World Development* **24** (5): 887–900.

Utting, Peter. 2007. CSR and equality. *Third World Quarterly* **28** (4): 697–712.

Valiyev, Anar M. 2006. Parliamentary elections in Azerbaijan: a failed revolution. *Problems of Post-Communism* **53** (3): 17–35.

Van der Linde, Claas. 1993. The microeconomic implication of environmental regulation: a preliminary framework. In *Environmental Policies and Industrial Competitiveness*. Paris: OECD, 69–77.

Van Dessel, J. P. 1995. The environmental situation in the Niger Delta. Internal position paper prepared for Greenpeace, Netherlands, February.

Vandewalle, Dirk. 1998. *Libya since Independence – Oil and State-Building*. New York: Cornell University Press.

Victor, David G. and Joshua C. House. 2006. BP's emissions trading system. *Energy Policy* **34** (15): 2100–12.

Ward, Halina, and Craig Smith. 2006. *Corporate Social Responsibility at a Crossroads: Futures for CSR in the UK to 2015*. London: International Institute for Environment and Development.

Warhurst, Alyson. 2001. Corporate citizenship and corporate social investment: drivers of tri-sector partnerships. *Journal of Corporate Citizenship* 1 (1): 57–73.

Warleigh, Alex. 2000. The hustle: citizenship practice, NGOs and 'policy coalitions' in the European Union – the cases of auto oil, drinking water and unit pricing. *Journal of European Public Policy* 7 (2): 229–43.

Welford, Richard. 2002. Globalization, corporate social responsibility and human rights. *Corporate Social Responsibility and Environmental Management* 9 (1): 1–7.

Wells, J. B., M. Perish and L. Guimaraes. 2001. Can oil and gas companies extend best operating practices to community development assistance programs? Paper read at SPE Asia Pacific Oil and Gas Conference and Exhibition, 17–19 April, at Jakarta, Indonesia.

Whelan, Glen. 2008. *A Rational Austrian Foundation for Management and Organization Studies*. ICCSR Research Paper Series 53. Nottingham: Nottingham University Business School.

White, Allen L. 2005. *Fade, Integrate or Transform? The Future of CSR*. San Francisco, CA: Business for Social Responsibility.

White, David and Andrew Jack. 2005. UN envoy calls on multinationals to help in Aids fight. *Financial Times*, 2 December.

White, S. 2002. Oil pollution: clearing up the myths. *Geography Review* 15 (5): 16–20.

Whitley, Richard. 1999. *Divergent Capitalisms: The Social Structuring and Change of Business Systems*. Oxford: Oxford University Press.

Wokutch, Richard E. 1990. Corporate social responsibility Japanese style. *Academy of Management Executive* 4 (2): 56–74.

Wood, Geoffrey and Jedrzej George Frynas. 2006. The institutional basis of economic failure: anatomy of the segmented business system. *Socio-Economic Review* 4 (2): 239–77.

World Bank. 2003. *Striking a Better Balance: The World Bank Group and Extractive Industries – Final Report of the Extractive Industries Review*, vol. I. Washington, DC: World Bank.

2004. *Regulation of Associated Gas Flaring and Venting: A Global Overview and Lessons*. Washington, DC: World Bank.

2008. World Bank statement on Chad–Cameroon pipeline. Press release 2009/073/AFR, 9 September.

World Commission on Environment and Development. 1987. *Our Common Future*. Oxford: Oxford University Press.

Wright, P. and S. Ferris. 1997. Agency conflict and corporate strategy: the effect of divestment on corporate value. *Strategic Management Journal* 18: 77–83.

Younger, S. 1992. Aid and the Dutch disease: macroeconomic management when everybody loves you. *World Development* 20 (11): 1587–97.

Zulkifli, Norhayah and Azlan Amran. 2006. Realizing corporate social responsibility in Malaysia. *Journal of Corporate Citizenship* (24): 101–14.

Zyglidopoulos, Stelios C. 2002. The social and environmental responsibilities of multinationals: evidence from the Brent Spar case. *Journal of Business Ethics* 36 (1/2): 141–51.

Index

LaVergne, TN USA
10 September 2010
196625LV00003B/42/P